Original story and screenplay written and directed by

HAYAO MIYAZAKI

PONYO

A young fish girl whom Sosuke named Ponyo. She loves Sosuke, and she also loves ham. She can use magic.

LISA

Sosuke's mother. She's been looking after Sosuke and Ponyo.

SOSUKE

A kind and polite five-year-old boy. He found Ponyo by the sea and has come to love her.

FUJIMOTO

Ponyo's father. He is studying how to reawaken the ancient seas.

GRAN MAMARE

Ponyo's mother. She is the Mother of the Sea and has magical powers.

TOKI

An old lady from the Sunflower Senior Center. She can be snappy but actually really likes Sosuke.

PREVIOUSLY

Ponyo transforms into a human and [illegible] with Sosuke. [illegible], Ponyo [illegible] herself human causes [illegible] the earth is now [illegible] water. [illegible] to find help, leaving Sosuke [illegible] Ponyo alone in the house on the cliff... [illegible] will happen next?

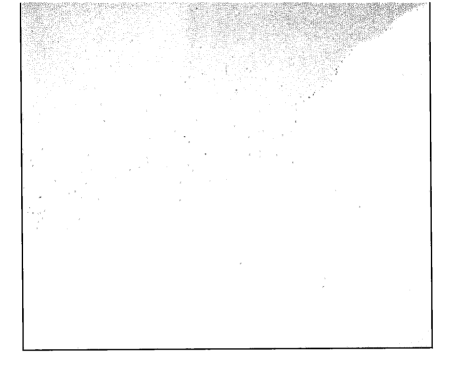

SOSUKE!
SOSUKE!
...!!
ゴチン

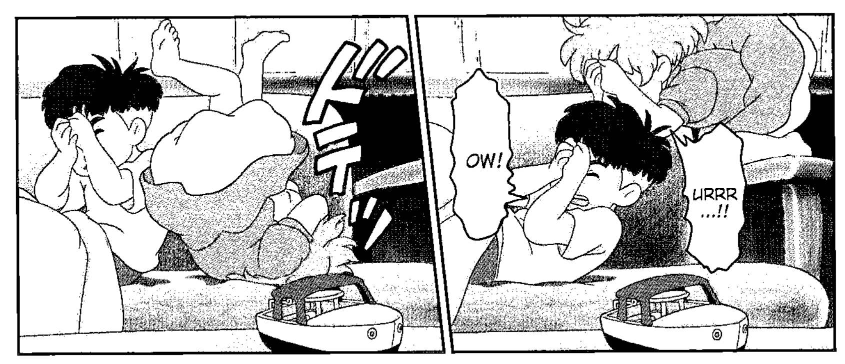
ドテッ
OW!
URRR ...!!

YOU OKAY?
PONYO !

GOOD MORN-ING...
...SO-SUKE!

カラララ

...!!

LOOK AT THAT, THE OCEAN IS AT OUR DOOR.

HOW COME YOUR MOM'S NOT HERE?

...?
TOO BAD WE DON'T HAVE A BOAT.
THE WATER'S SO HIGH, SHE MUST BE STUCK.

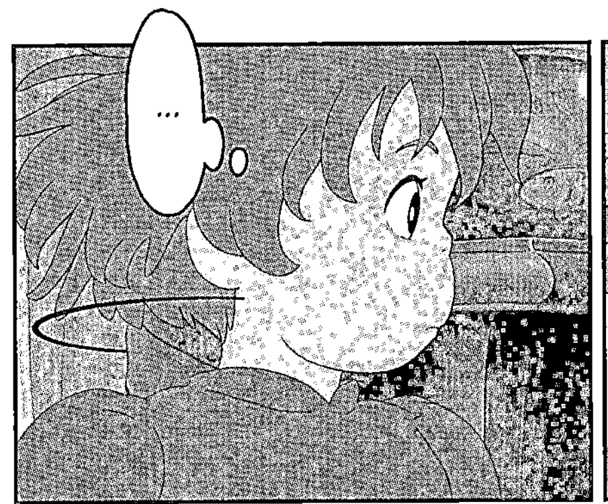
...

THERE'S A BOAT RIGHT THERE.

IT'S A LITTLE SMALL.

NO, IT'S NOT.

GGHHH...

URR...

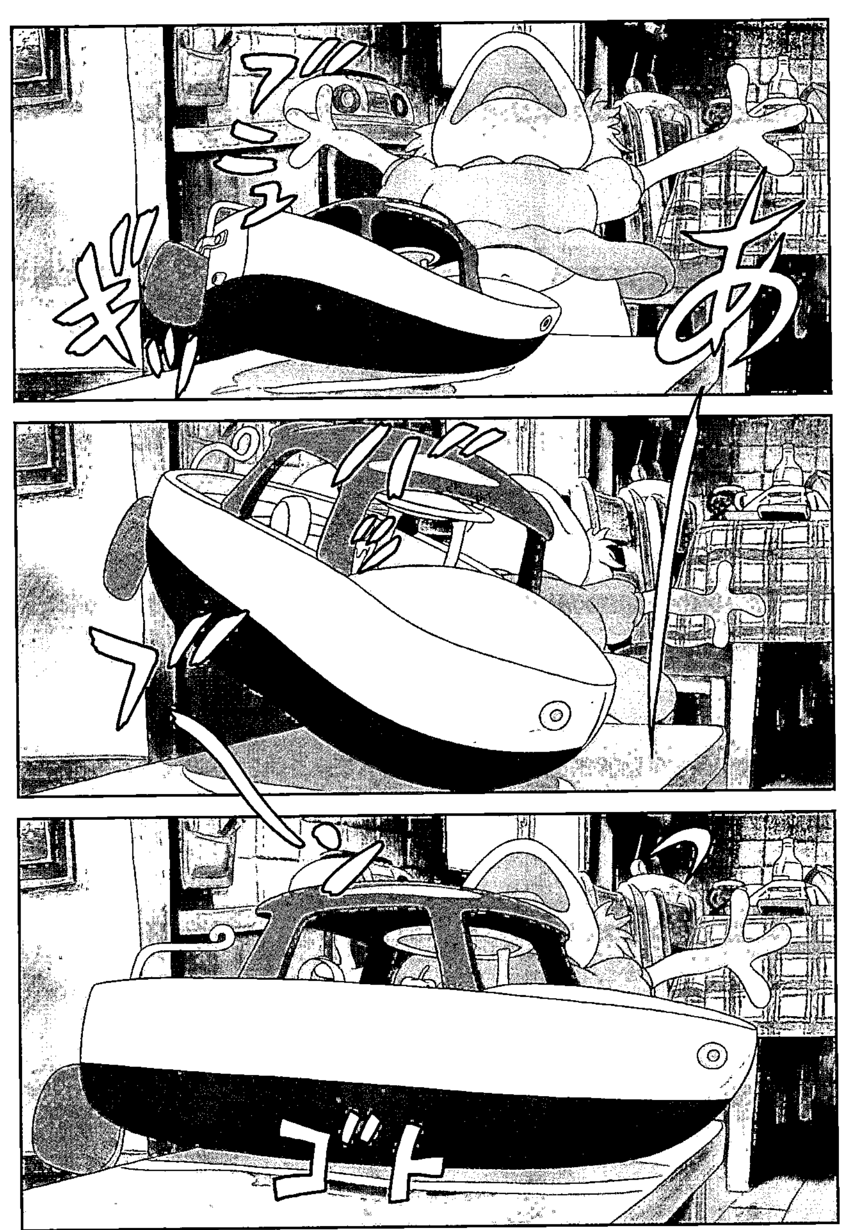

あ
ブニュ
ゴト

...!!

ニカ〜ッ

THANK YOU!

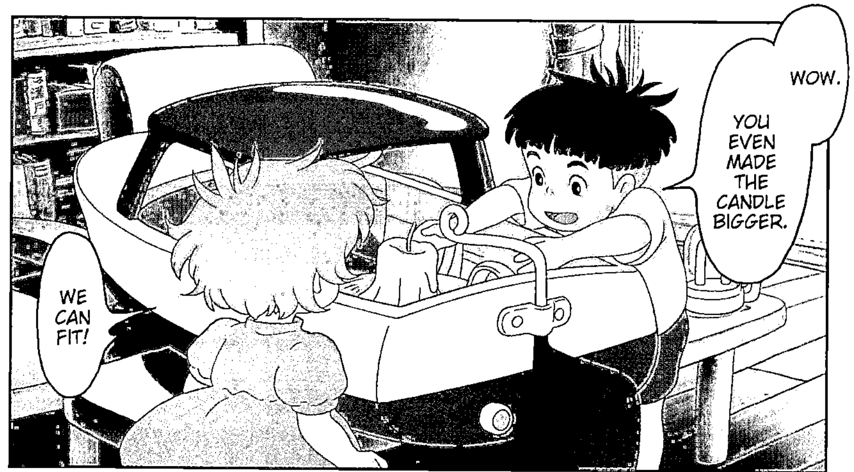
WOW.
YOU EVEN MADE THE CANDLE BIGGER.
WE CAN FIT!

GRAB THAT END, PLEASE.
OKAY.

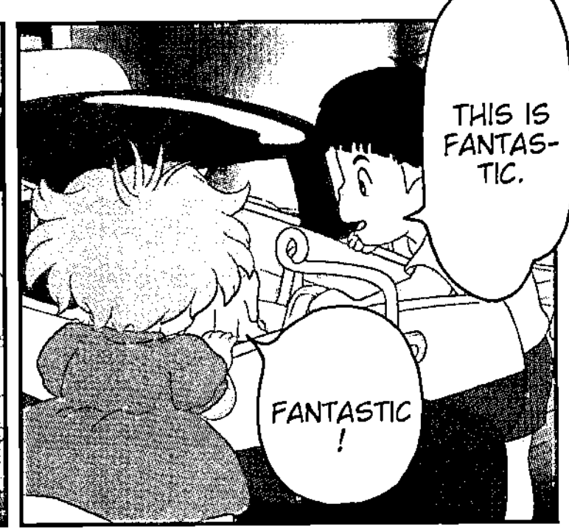
THIS IS FANTAS-TIC.
FANTASTIC!

LET'S GO!

READY?

WHOA!

ダダッ

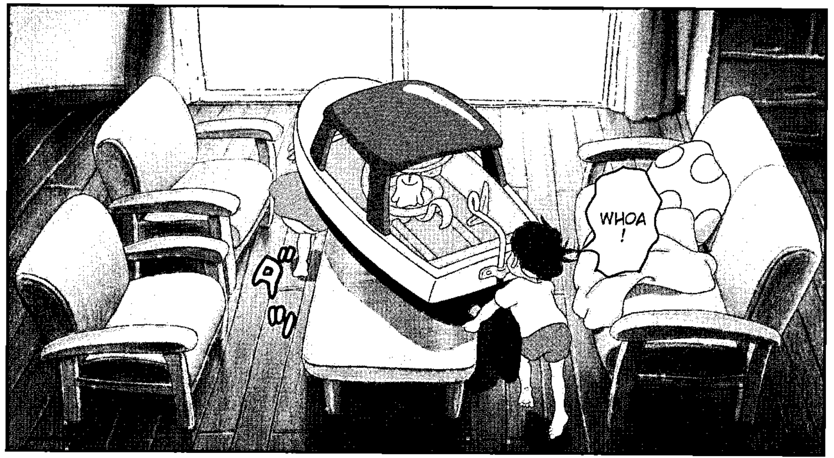
WHOA!
ダッ

WHOA!

WHOA!

AH!
ザブ
ザブ

バシャーン

IT ACTUALLY FLOATS!

DOESN'T LOOK LIKE IT HAS ANY LEAKS.

NOW WE HAVE TO FILL THE BOILER.

...?

THE WATER GETS SUCKED IN THROUGH THIS PIPE.

THEN IT GETS HEATED UP HERE IN THE BOILER.
...?

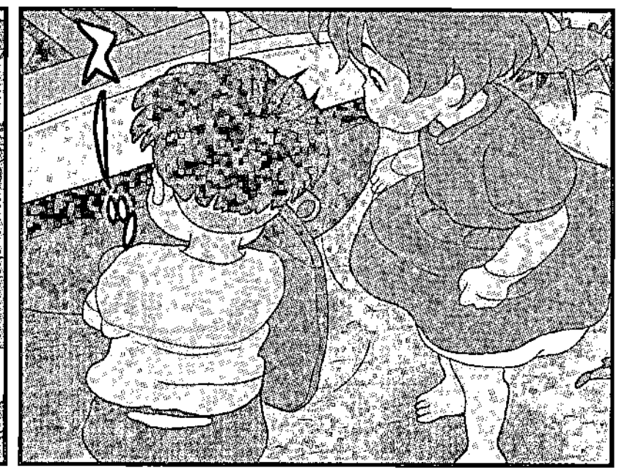

HMM
...

ポチャッ

フゥ

ちゃぽん

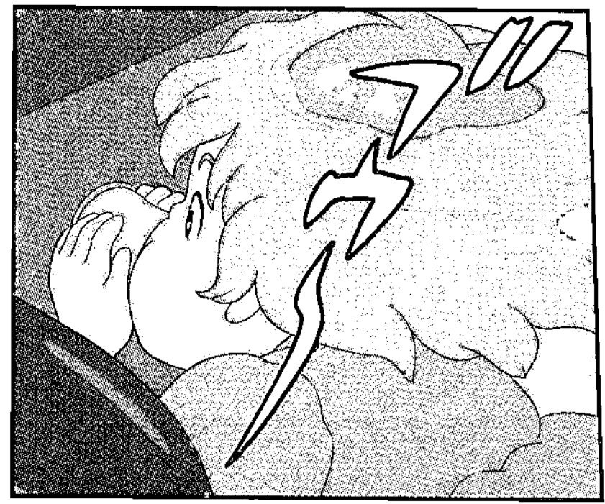
ブウ

ベコン・・!!

HAAA!

WELL ...
...THAT WORKED!

チャポッ

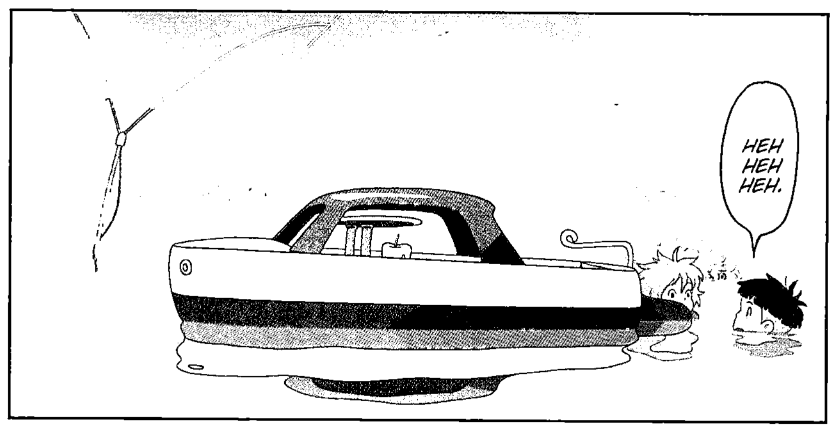
HEH HEH HEH.

LOOKS LIKE EVERY-THING'S SHIP-SHAPE.

HA HA HA.

SHIP-SHAPE?
YEP.

SHIP-SHAPE!
SHIP-SHAPE!

SHIP-SHAPE!
SHIP-SHAPE?

ガサ..

ゴソ..

グッ

キリッ

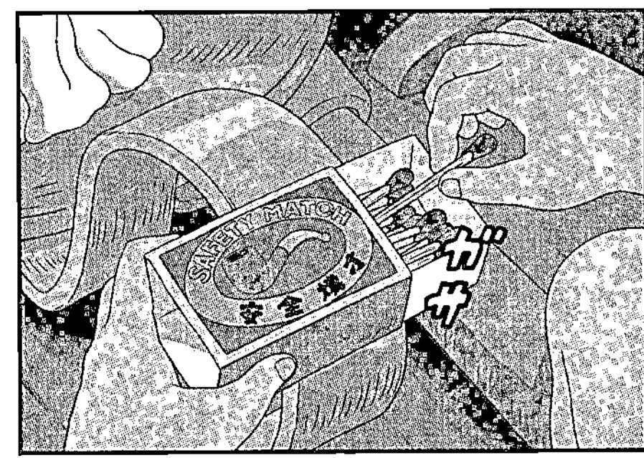
SAFETY MATCH
ガサ

IS IT HOT?

IT'S HOT!

OW!

OW!

LOOK AT THAT!

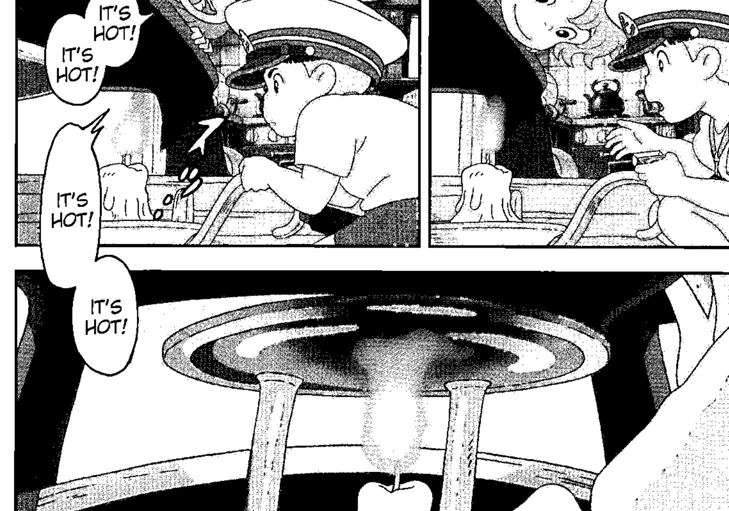
IT'S BURNING!
IT'S HOT!
IT'S HOT!
IT'S HOT!
IT'S HOT!

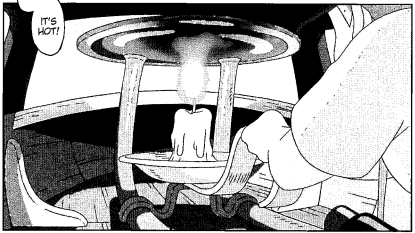

IT'S HOT, ISN'T IT?
...

HMM...

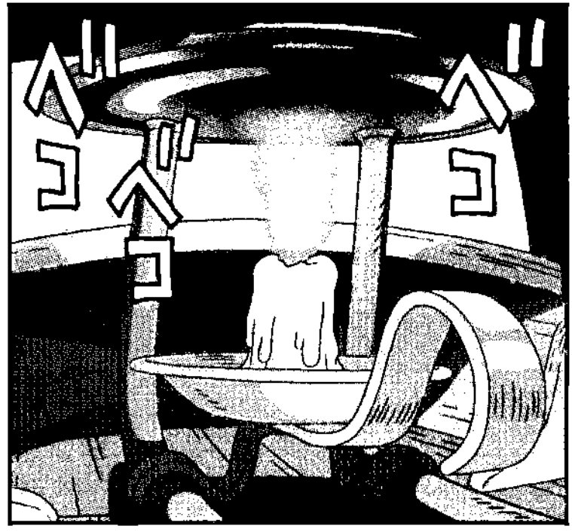
ベコ
ベコ
ベコ

ベコ
ベコ
ベコ

IT WORKS!
ベコ
ベコ
ベコ

テケ
テケ
テケ

SOSUKE ...
WE'RE SHIP-SHAPE, RIGHT?
テケ
テケ
MM-HM.

THIS IS A GOOD BOAT.
テケ
テケ
MM-HM.

テケ テケ テケ

HEY, SOSUKE, LOOK AT ME!
MM-HM.
テケ テケ テケ

SOSUKE, WE'RE MOVING, AREN'T WE?
MM-HM.

テケ テケ
SOSUKE, IT'S REALLY HOT, ISN'T IT?

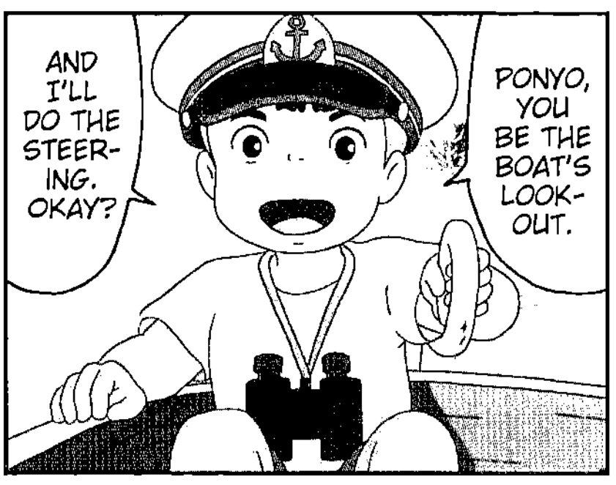
PONYO, YOU BE THE BOAT'S LOOK-OUT.
AND I'LL DO THE STEER-ING. OKAY?

テケ
テケ
OKAY.
I'M THE LOOK-OUT!

テケ
テケ
テケ

テケ
テケ
テケ

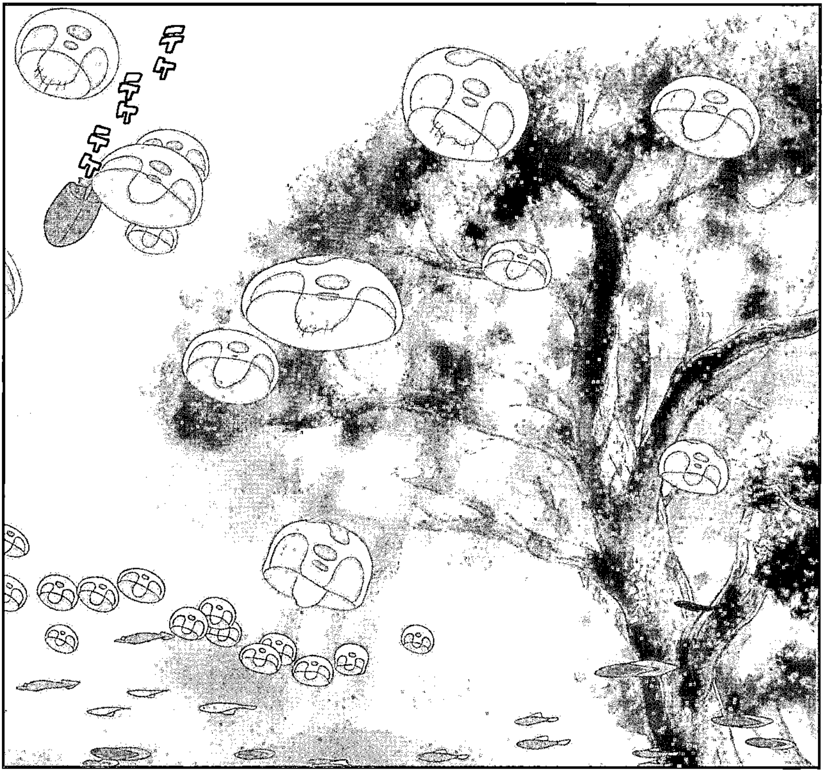

テケ
テケ
テケ

THAT'S THE ROAD MY MOM TOOK LAST NIGHT.

THERE'S THE ROAD.

I DON'T SEE HER ANY-WHERE.
WE'LL SEE HER.
SHE PROMISED ME SHE'D COME BACK.

THOSE ARE ANCIENT FISH...
THEY LIVED DURING THE DEVONIAN AGE.
THAT'S A BOTHRIO-LEPIS.

AND THAT ONE IS...
DIPNORHYNCHUS!
DIPNORHYNCHUS!

WOW. THAT ONE'S REALLY HUGE.

THAT'S DEVO-NYN-CHUS.
DEVO-NYN-CHUS.

AHOY THERE!
AHOY!
AHOY!
THERE'S A BOAT!
AHOY!
I'M GONNA SAY THAT.
テケ テケ
AHOY!
テケ テケ

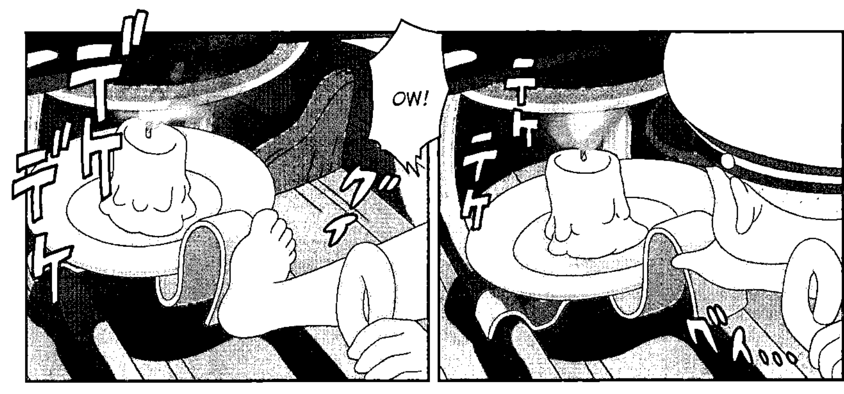
OW!

WHOA!
THAT'S FAST!

I'M GETTING THE HANG OF THIS.

PREPARE TO STOP, PONYO.

HELLO, YOU TWO.
HELLO.
THAT'S QUITE A BOAT YOU'VE GOT THERE.

YOU'RE LISA'S LITTLE BOY, AREN'T YOU?

THAT'S PONYO.
HE'S SO-SUKE.
HE'S NOT A LITTLE BOY.

I...
...USED TO BE A FISH.

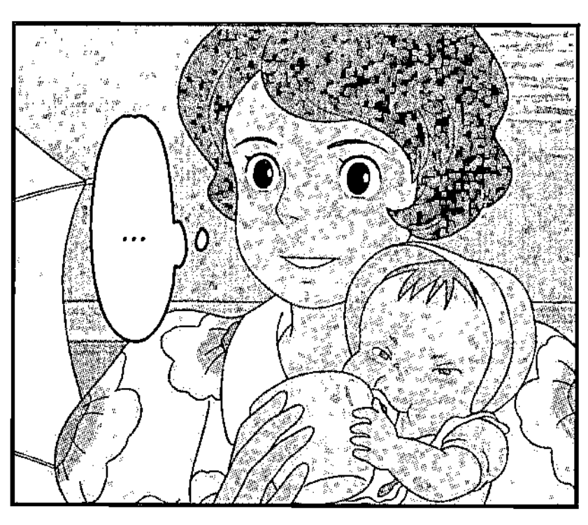
...

LET ME HAVE THE CUP, SWEETIE.

ポタ

YOU'RE LISA'S LITTLE BOY, AREN'T YOU?

THAT'S PONYO.
HE'S NOT A LITTLE BOY.
HE'S SO-SUKE.

I...
...USED TO BE A FISH.

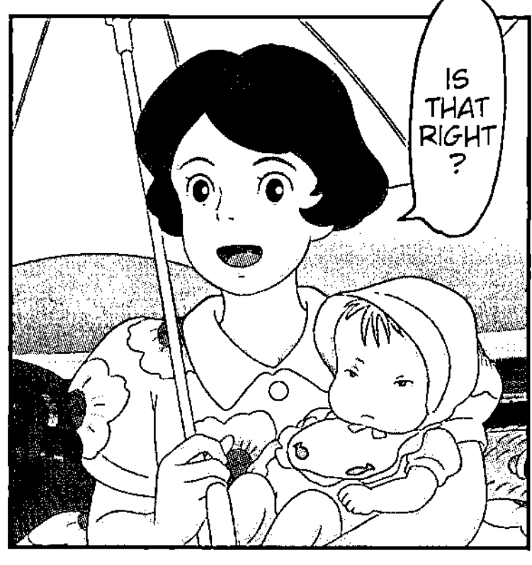
IS THAT RIGHT ?

...

I LIKE YOUR NAME, PONYO. IT'S CUTE.

...?!
YOUR MOTHER ?

BY THE WAY, HAVE YOU SEEN MY MOM?

WHY ISN'T YOUR MOTHER WITH YOU?
SHE WENT TO THE SENIOR CENTER.

MY BABY LIKES YOU.

OH, DID SHE?

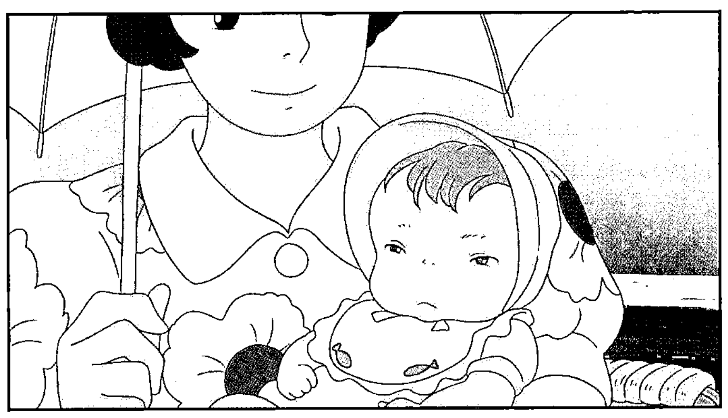

...
...

...
...

OH, SWEETHEART. WHAT'S THE MATTER?

...?!

HMM ...
OH, IS THAT FOR US?

...

LET ME HAVE THE CUP, SWEETIE.

ポタ

ドボドボ

YUM, IS THAT SOUP?

IT SMELLS GOOD.

IT'S DELICIOUS, PONYO.
THANK YOU.
あう
あう

MY MOM MADE IT FROM SCRATCH.

THE SOUP'S FOR HIM.

OH, I'M SORRY. HE'S A LITTLE TOO YOUNG, HE CAN'T HANDLE SOUP YET.
BUT I COULD EAT THE SOUP INSTEAD, AND IT WOULD HELP ME MAKE MILK FOR HIM.

MY MOM MADE MILK FOR ME TOO.
HMM.

IS IT ALL RIGHT IF I EAT THIS SOUP?
PONYO, WHAT DO YOU SAY?

THANK YOU, SWEET-HEART.
...?!

THAT'S FINE.

エイッ
エイッ
大漁
浦水産高校
AHOY!
ARE ANY OF YOU IN NEED OF ASSISTANCE AT THIS TIME?
PEOPLE FROM THE TOWN.
IT'S LIKE A PARADE.
WE'RE ALL GOOD HERE.
BUT THANKS FOR CHECKING ON US, CAPTAIN.

WE'RE FERRYING EVERYONE TO THE MOUNTAIN PEAK HOTEL. FOR YOUR SAFETY, WE'D REQUEST THAT YOU FOLLOW US.
AYE-AYE, WILL DO.

LOOKS LIKE THE WHOLE TOWN IS HERE.
I DON'T SEE YOUR MOM.
I HOPE SHE'S OKAY.

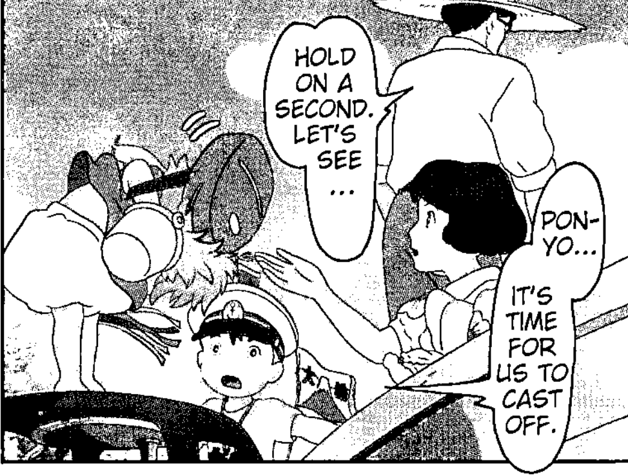
PON-YO...
IT'S TIME FOR US TO CAST OFF.
HOLD ON A SECOND. LET'S SEE ...

HERE, HAVE SOME MILK.

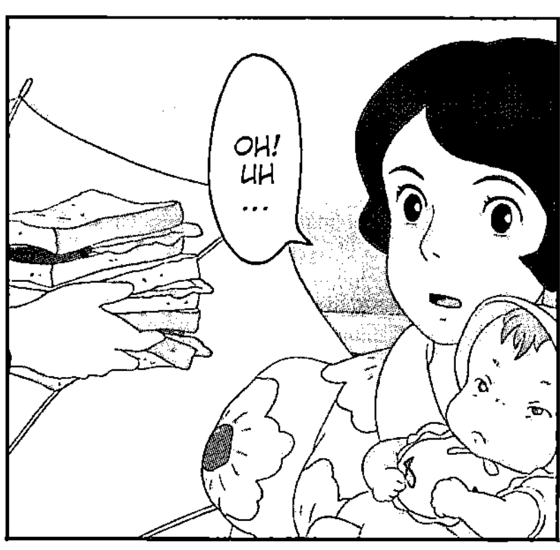
OH! UH ...

IT'S FOR MILK!
テケテケ
テケ
テケ

SHE ALREADY ATE ALL THE HAM OFF THOSE SAND-WICHES.
テケテケ

THANK YOU.
THAT'S VERY GENEROUS OF YOU, PONYO.

HERE, SO-SUKE.
I BROUGHT YOU OUR BIGGEST CANDLE.
THANKS.
PONYO WILL MAKE IT BIGGER.
SEE YOU LATER!
TAKE CARE!
テケ テケ
BE CARE-FUL!
テケ テケ
ウエ～ン
ヒック ヒック

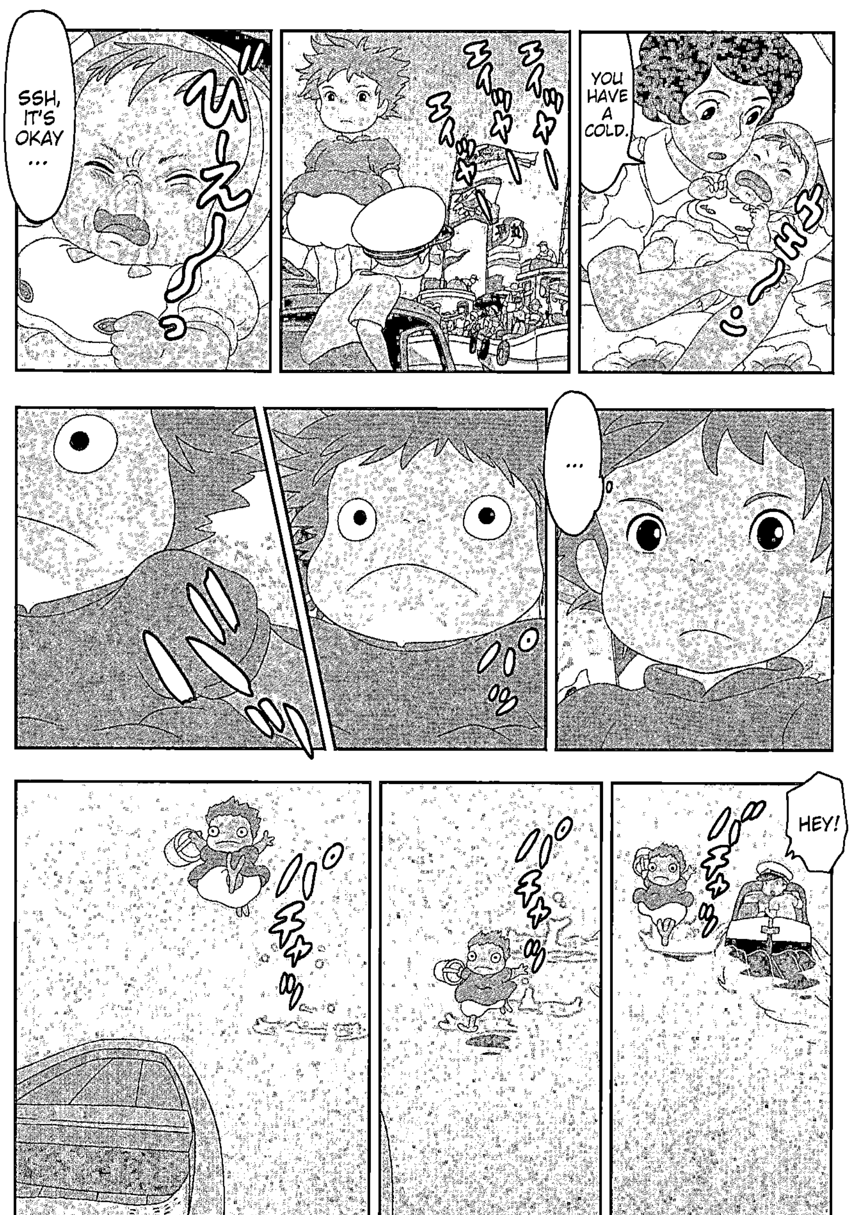
SSH, IT'S OKAY...
YOU HAVE A COLD.
...
HEY!

タタタ

トン

HUPP !!
びたっ
ウェーン
ダッ

ぎゅ～っ
ぐりぐり

...
ニカッ

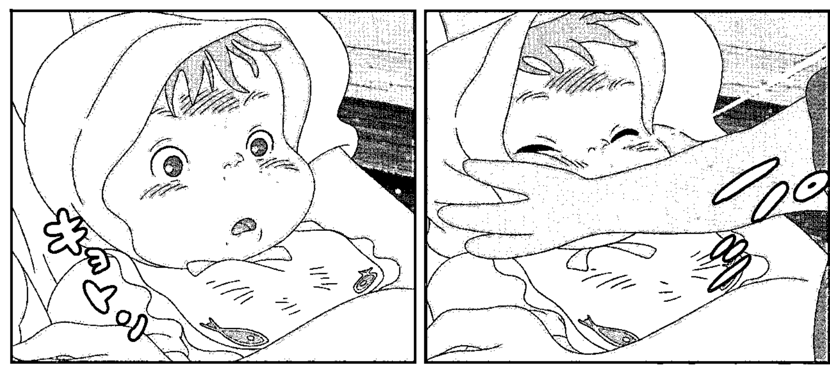
キョトッ

PON-
YO!

WHA
...
アウー
アウ

テケテケテケ

SOSU-KE!
HEY, SOSU-KE!
WOW!
NICE BOAT!
WHERE'S YOUR MOTHER?
テケテケテケ

YOU SHOULDN'T BE OUT HERE ALONE.
SHE WENT TO THE SENIOR CENTER LAST NIGHT. WE'RE ON OUR WAY TO FIND HER.

YEAH, THAT'S LISA!
I CAN'T BELIEVE YOUR MOTHER BEAT THAT WAVE!

I CAN'T. I'M BUSY. I HAVE A JOB.

SOSUKE!
CAN I RIDE WITH YOU?

YOU'LL FIND HER!
GOOD LUCK, KID!
CHECK THE PARK. THE SENIORS SHOULD HAVE EVACUATED TO THERE.

WE'LL SEND A BOAT FOR THE SENIORS AS SOON AS WE DROP THIS GROUP OFF.
GOOD LUCK, CAP-TAIN!

テケ テケ テケ

テケ テケ テケ...

クエー
テケテケ
テケ
テケ

テケッ…
テケッ…
テケッ…
テケッ…
テケッ

PONYO. OUR CANDLE IS ABOUT OUT.
コクリ。。

トローン

グリ
グリ

...

WE'LL BE OKAY. THE FISHERMAN GAVE ME ANOTHER ONE.

OW!
IT'S STILL PRETTY HOT.

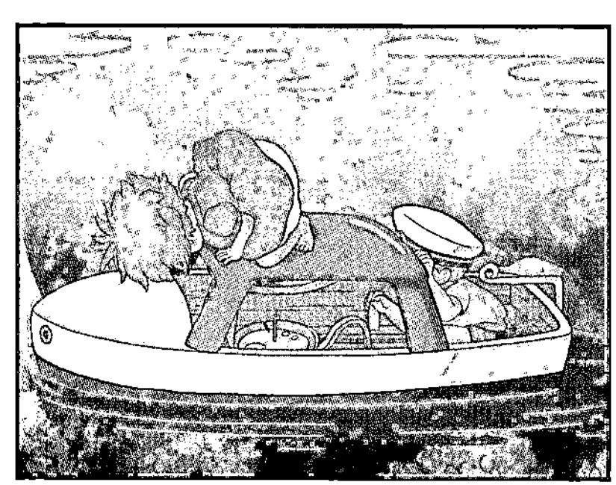

BYE-BYE.

HERE, PONYO.
CAN YOU MAKE THIS BIGGER?

HM?
ALL RIGHT.

HEY.
ARE YOU OKAY?

MM.

URR
...

HM?

PONYO
?

PONYO!

PONYO!

チャポーン

チャプ

バシャ
バシャ

OH GOOD, I CAN WALK FROM HERE.

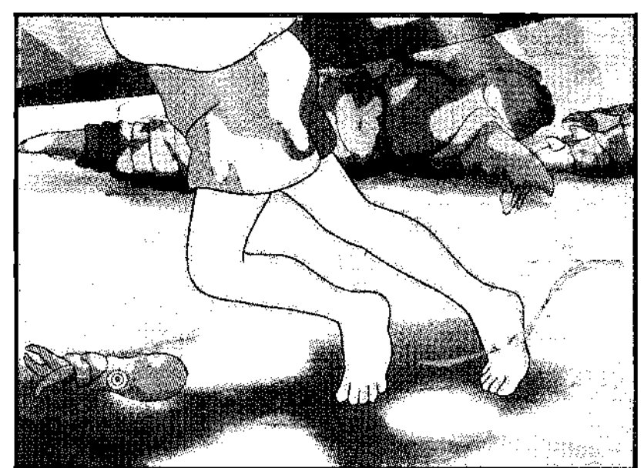

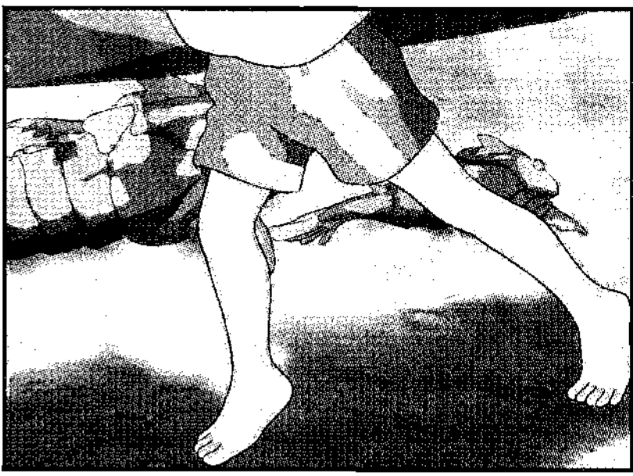

THERE'S THE ROAD.

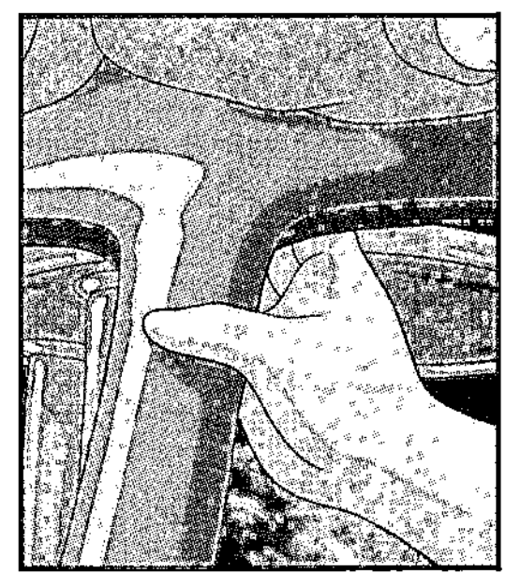

HEY!!

...?!
IT'S SHRINK-ING!

THE BOAT!

PONYO !!

ザブ
ハァ
ハァ

バシャ
バシャ

ハァ
ハァ
バシャ
バシャ

ドタッ!
ズルッ

ドボン

ハァ
ハァ
ハァ
へ

PONYO!
PONYO, WAKE UP!
す

SO-SUKE...

ゴシゴシ

ふあ

...?!

YOU SCARED ME. DON'T TURN INTO A FISH AGAIN—I'D HATE IT.

...!!

MY MOM'S CAR!

PONYO, COME ON.

...

SHE MIGHT BE THERE!

HEY, MOM!
MOM?
RRR...
333

333

MOM?
TISSUES

MOMMY!

MOM!

MOMMY!

MOM!

MOMMY?

MOM!

HEY, MOM!

HPP ...
HPP ...

ペタ
ペタ

ペタ
ペタ

THERE'S WATER COMING FROM YOUR EYES.

HERE, I'VE GOT YOUR BOAT.

LET'S GO FIND YOUR MOM.

MM-
HMM.

40

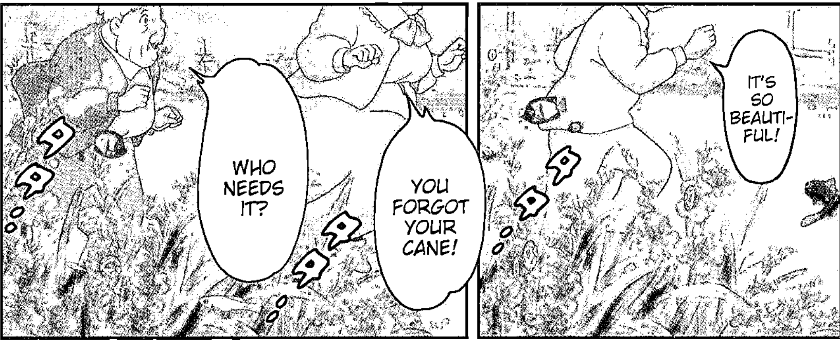
IT'S SO BEAUTI-FUL!
YOU FORGOT YOUR CANE!
WHO NEEDS IT?

HERE COMES THE WHALE AGAIN!
MY GOODNESS.
HE'S SO BIG.
THIS IS SO EXCITING!
HIS EYES ARE SO GENTLE.
I THINK HE SEES US.
THE "OTHER SIDE" IS NICE, ISN'T IT?
AND MY KNEES DON'T HURT.
WE DIDN'T NEED TO BE AFRAID.
YOU MEAN THIS IS THE OTHER SIDE?
WHERE DO YOU THINK WE ARE, LAS VEGAS?
IT'S LIKE A DREAM.

LADIES!
GATHER ROUND, PLEASE!
COMING!
LET'S GO!
IT'S SO NICE TO RUN.
RUN!
SPEED!

…

NOW I DON'T BELIEVE HIM.
WHAT DOES LISA THINK?

SHE'S WITH THAT WOMAN.
THEY'VE BEEN TALKING ALL NIGHT.

LADIES!
GATHER ROUND, PLEASE!
COMING!
LET'S GO!
IT'S SO NICE TO RUN.
SPEED!
RUN!

NO FAIR!

BEAT YOU THERE.

GOLD!
KAYO, WHO KNEW?

HYA!
KYA!

QUIET, PLEASE.
EVERY-ONE!

...

THE TIME HAS COME FOR YOU TO BEAR WIT-NESS.
TO A SACRED TEST OF LOVE.
ARE WE TOO OLD?
IT'S A TRIAL OF LOVE.
OH! EXCITING!
ARE THEY IN DANGER?

THE CHILDREN ARE COMING NOW...

PLEASE, LADIES.
HOW RO-MAN-TIC!

YOU WON'T LET ANY HARM COME TO SOSUKE OR PONYO NOW, WILL YOU?
FUJI-MOTO ...

AND THIS IS A VERY IMPORTANT MOMENT.

WE CAN PROTECT THEM IF HE ...
HE'S A WING NUT.
I BELIEVE IN HIM, DON'T YOU?
HE MIGHT.
IT'S NOT IN HIS NA-TURE.

EXCUSE ME.

OF COURSE I WOULD NOT!
I HOPE PONYO WILL STAY ASLEEP.

...

NOW I DON'T BELIEVE HIM.
WHAT DOES LISA THINK?

SHE'S WITH THAT WOMAN.
THEY'VE BEEN TALKING ALL NIGHT.

I WISH WE COULD HEAR WHAT THEY'RE TALKING ABOUT.
POOR LISA.

LISA!
LISA? ARE YOU ALL RIGHT?

WHY DON'T WE JUST ASK?

WE'RE ALL ON SOSUKE AND PONYO'S SIDE!!

...

MY DEAR!
WHAT'S GOING ON?
HE IS AN OLD SOUL.
THAT'S RIGHT.
SO-SUKE IS A STRONG BOY.
DO YOU NEED US?
PLEASE DON'T WORRY.

WE LOVE HIM.
WE'RE HERE.
OF COURSE YOU DO.

I WISH HIS FATHER WAS HERE.
THANK YOU.

...!

LOOK, IT'S A TUNNEL.

止まれ

DON'T LET GO OF MY HAND.
MM.

PONYO?

DON'T LIKE THIS PLACE.

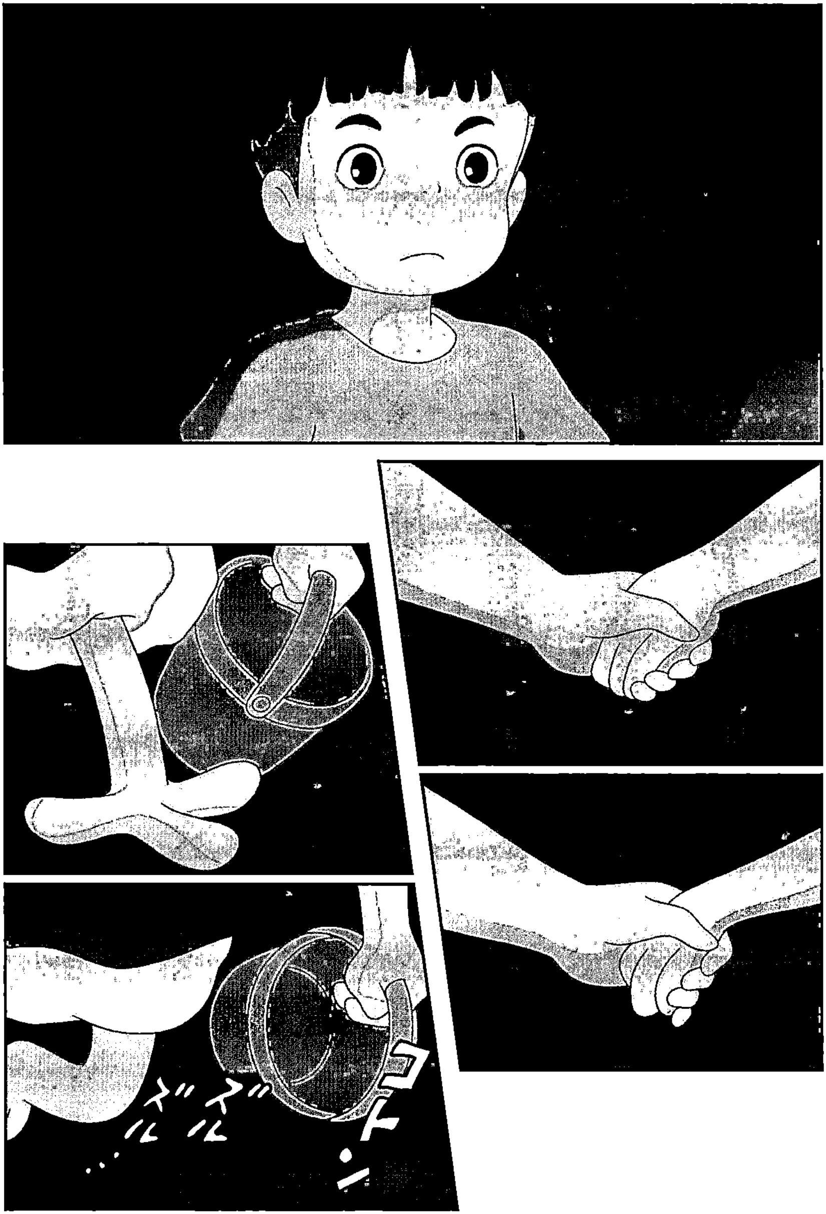

コト・ン

ズルズル…

!
PONYO !

PONYO !
ヘメヘメ…

PONYO !

ハァ
ハァ
タタタ…

ハァ
ハァ
タタ

タタタ…

PONYO !

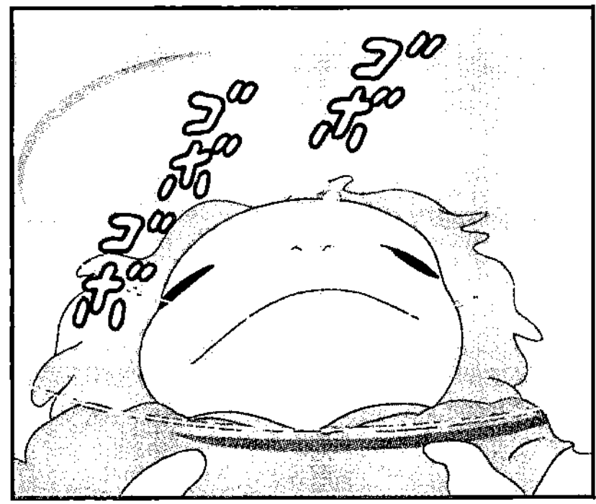
ゴボ
ゴボ
ゴボ

くーっ

PONYO!
ユサ
ユサ

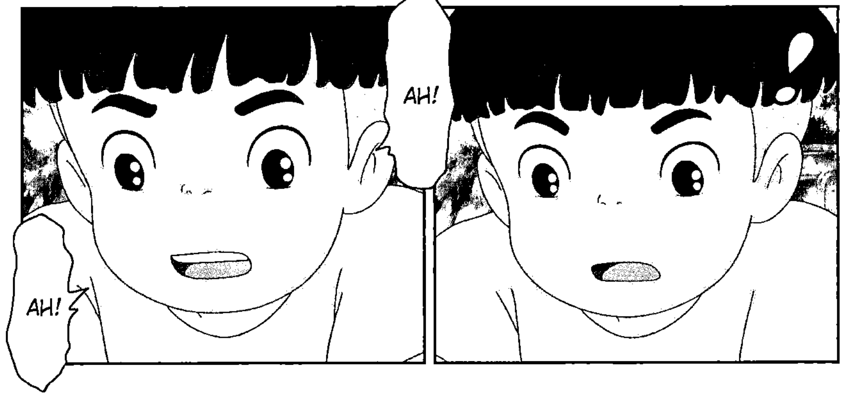
AH!
AH!

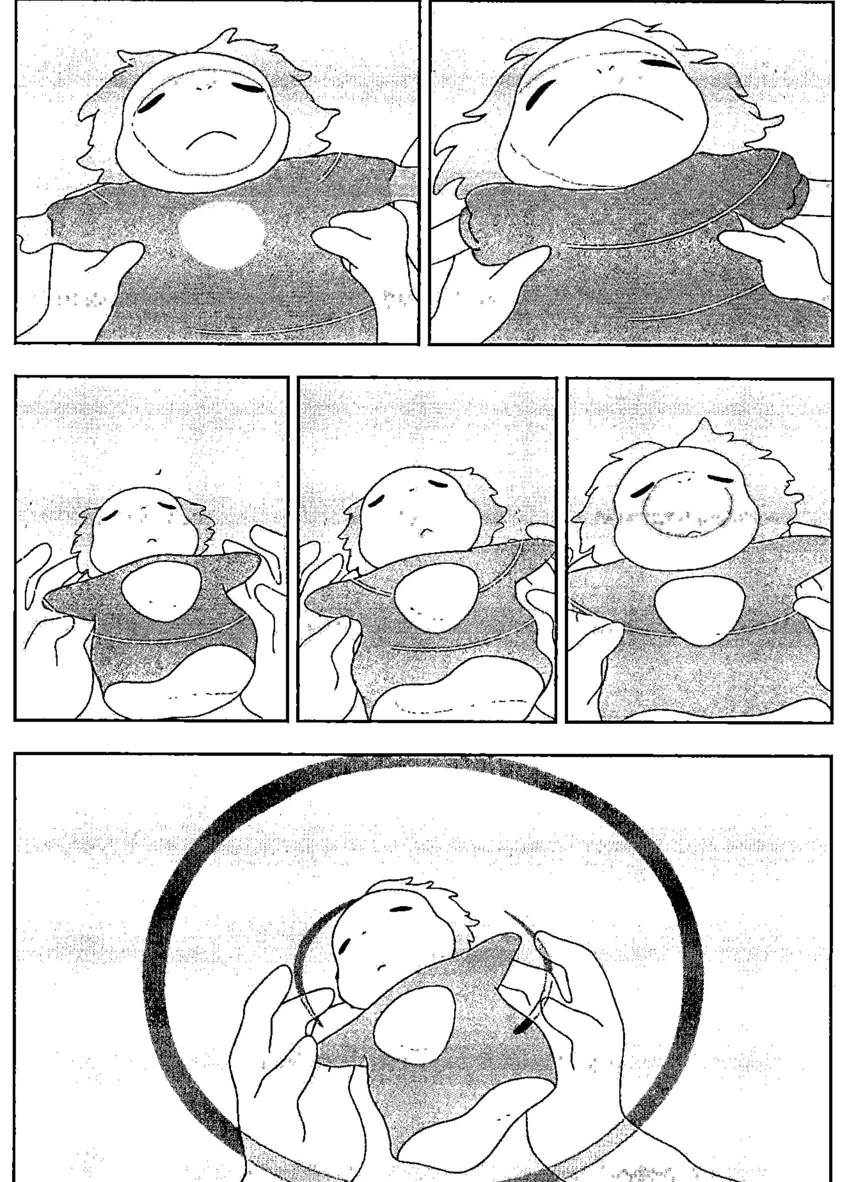

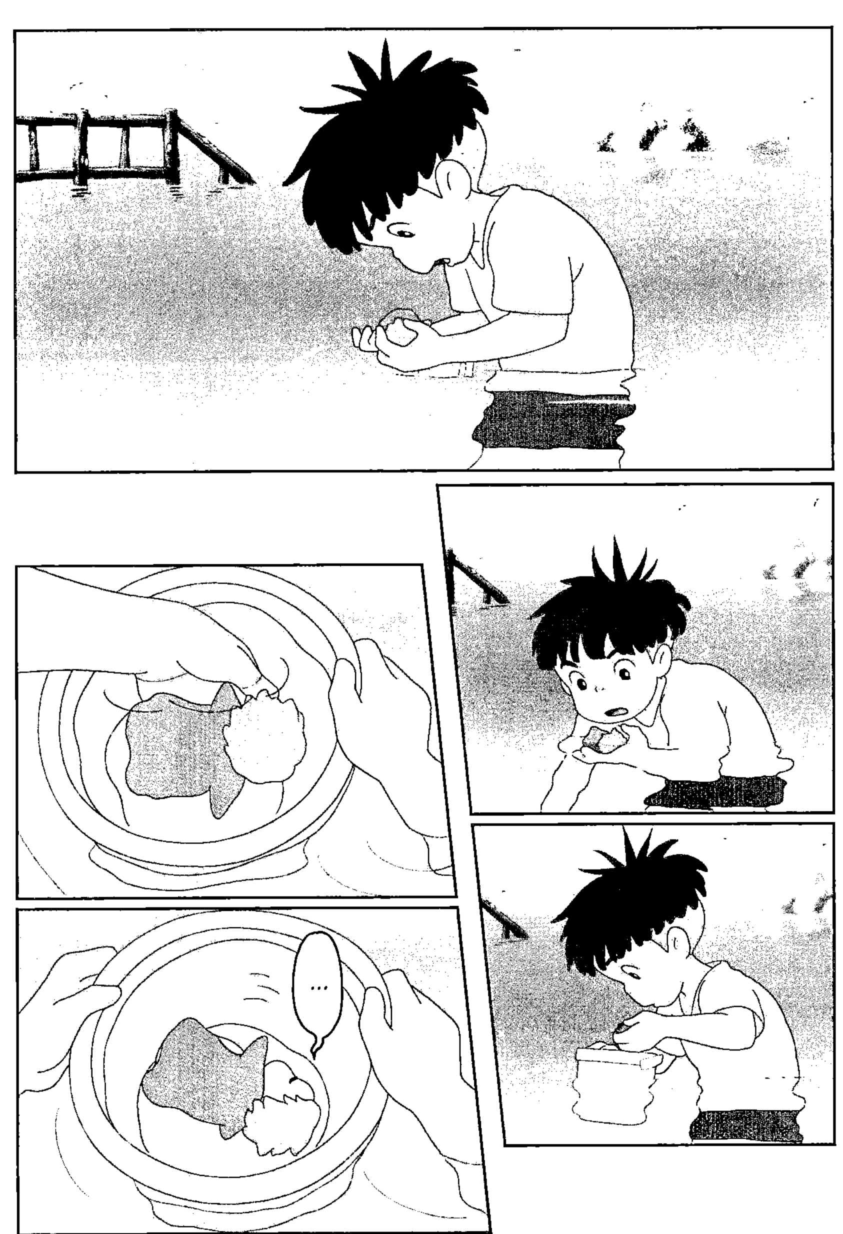

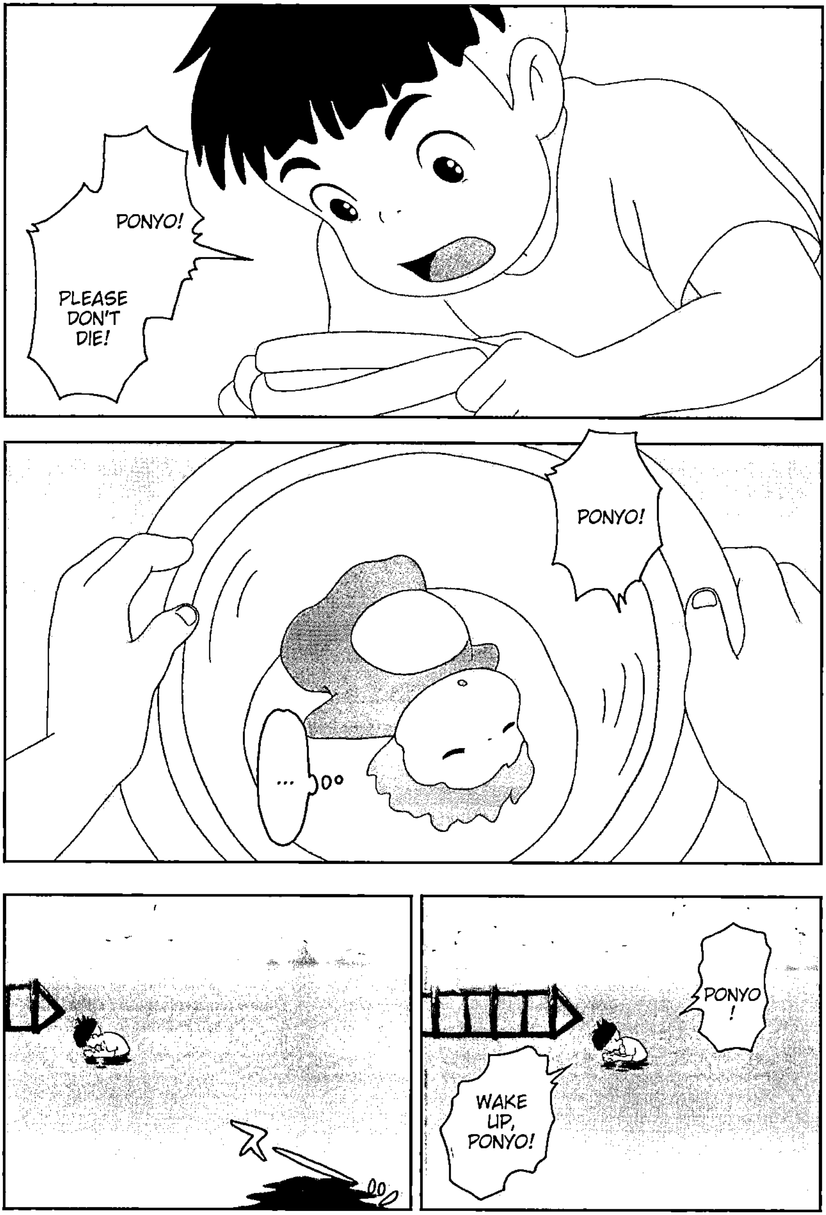

PONYO!
PLEASE DON'T DIE!

PONYO!

...

...?!
SHHH.
DON'T WAKE HER.

I'M GLAD TO MEET YOU, SOSUKE.
WE'VE ALL BEEN WAITING FOR YOU—YOUR MOTHER, THOSE OLD LADIES, YOUR FRIENDS.

WON'T YOU COME WITH ME AND JOIN THEM?
PONYO TOO.

...
MY MOM ?

...!!

COME WITH ME. I'M NOT GOING TO TAKE PONYO FROM YOU.
COME WITH ME.

SOSUKE!

...?!
...?!

SOSUKE, DON'T LISTEN TO THAT WACKO.

HE TRICKED ALL THE OTHERS INTO GOING WITH HIM.

TOKI!

BUT HE COULDN'T FOOL ME THOUGH.

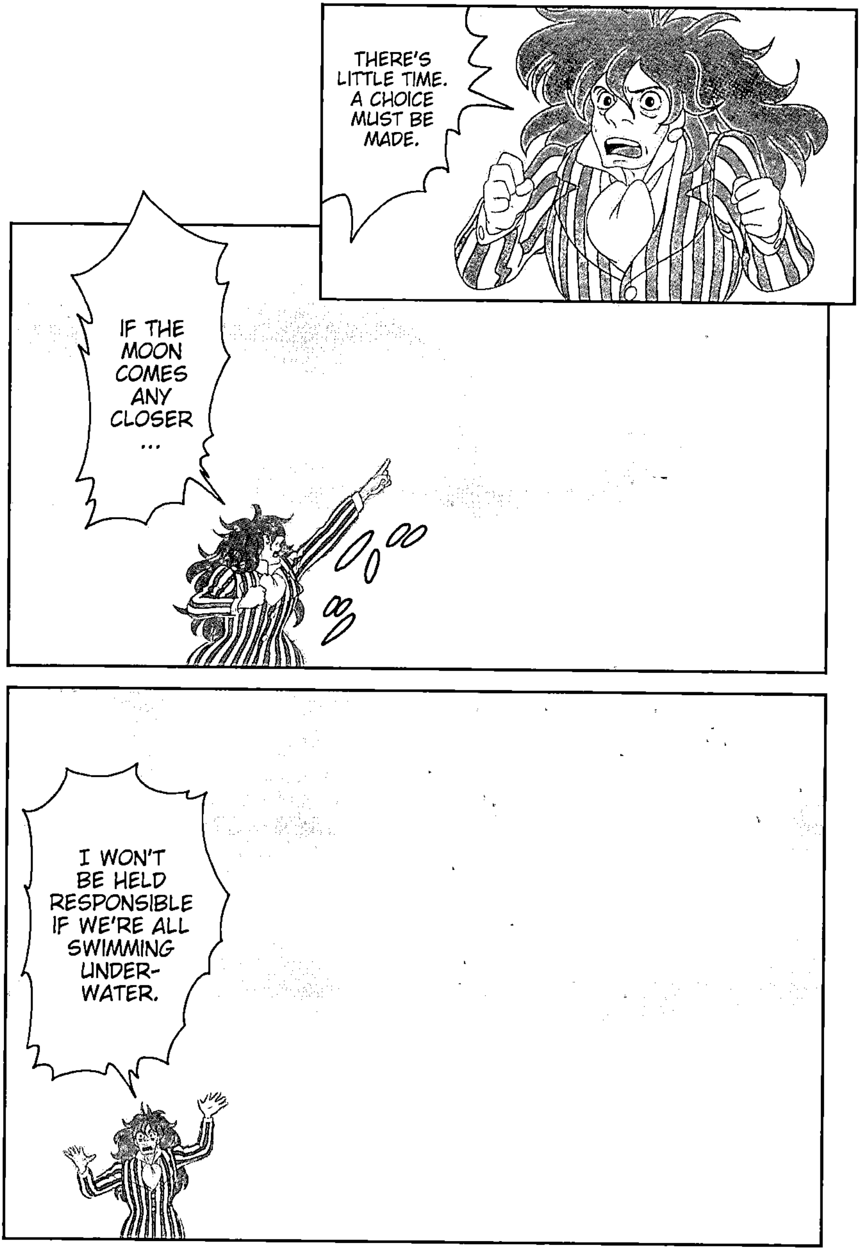

THERE'S LITTLE TIME. A CHOICE MUST BE MADE.
IF THE MOON COMES ANY CLOSER ...
I WON'T BE HELD RESPONSIBLE IF WE'RE ALL SWIMMING UNDER-WATER.

SO THAT'S THE BEST YOU CAN COME UP WITH? A FALLING MOON?

ARGH!
HUMANS!
SOSUKE, COME TO ME!

...

SOSUKE...
PLEASE LISTEN TO ME.

YOU'RE THE ONLY ONE WHO CAN SAVE THE PLANET!

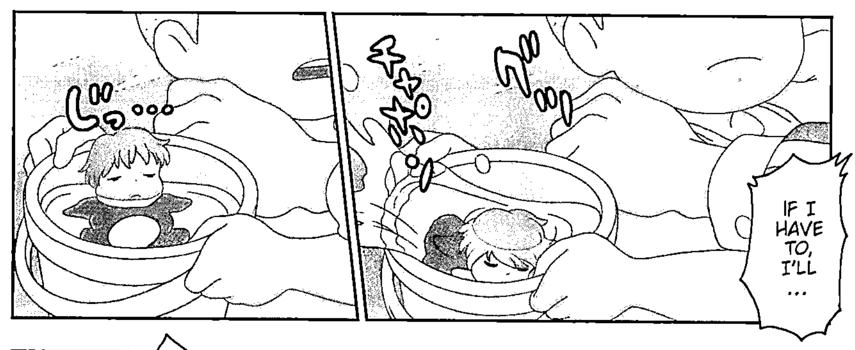
IF I HAVE TO, I'LL ...

...!!

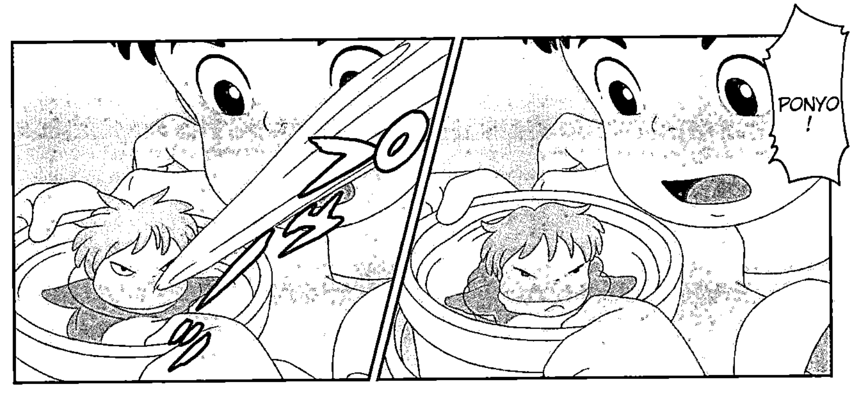

BRUN-
HILDE?!

タタタタタ

チャプ
チャプ
PONYO
!

HURRY!
ヨロ ヨロ
COME TO ME!
ガク ガク

I DON'T UNDER-STAND!

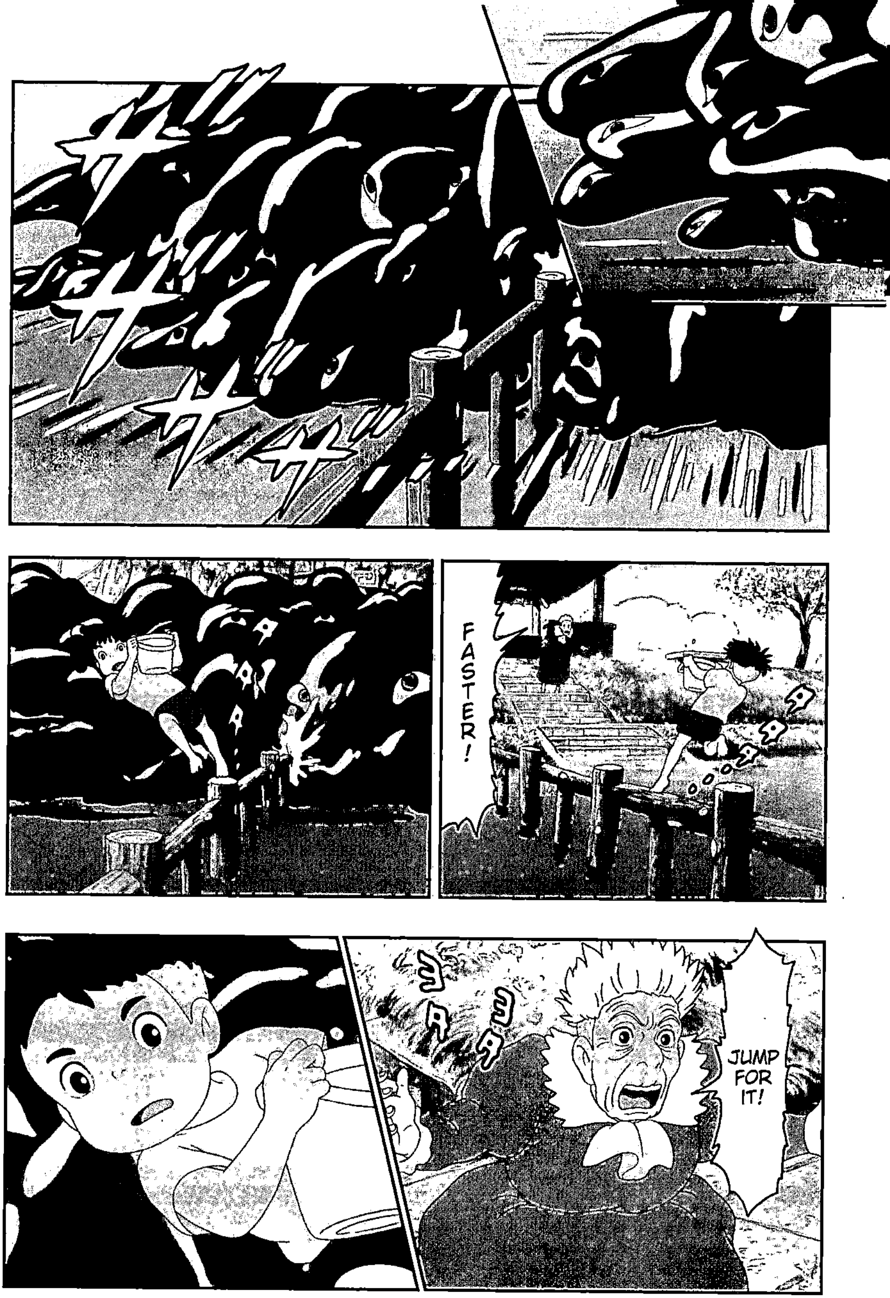

FASTER!
タタタ

ヨタヨタ
JUMP FOR IT!

ガシッ

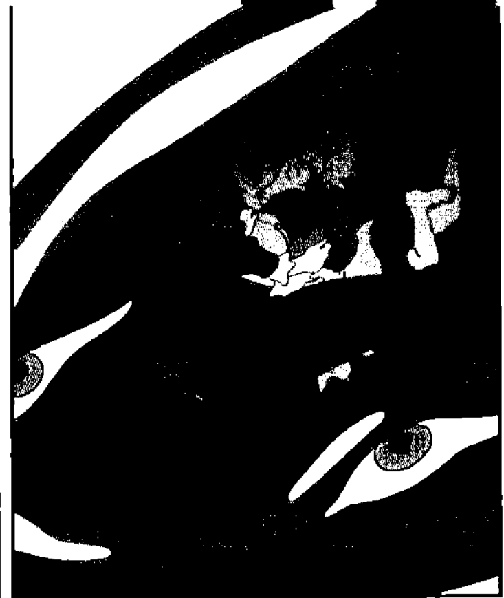

OH, WHAT NOW?

...!!

...

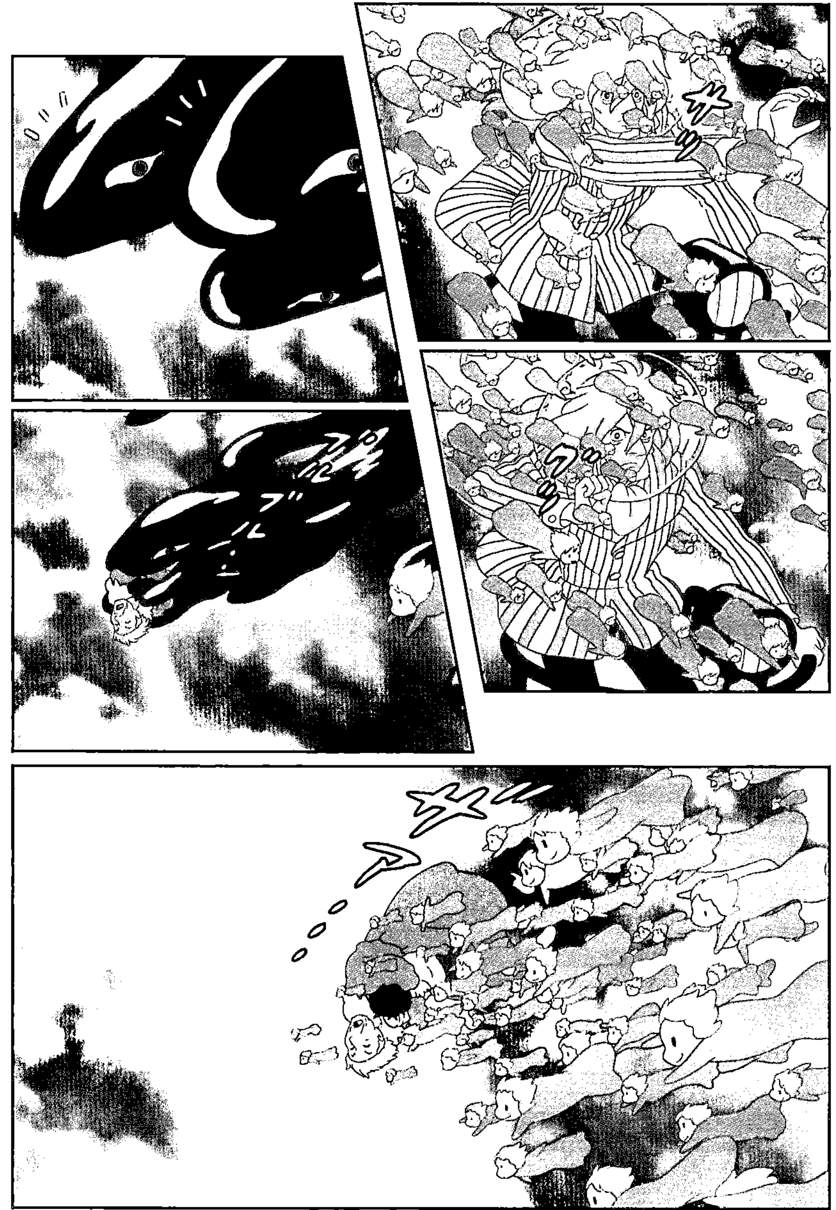
プルブル…
グッ

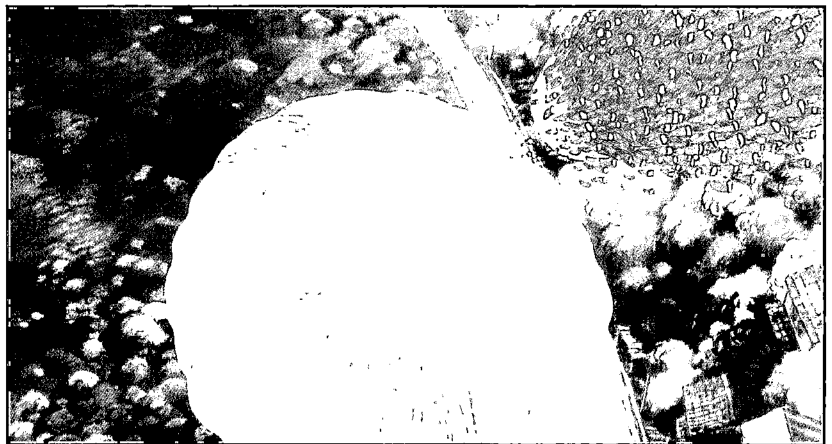

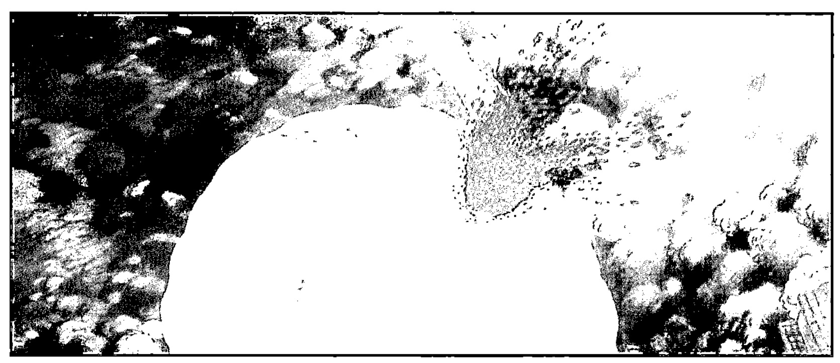

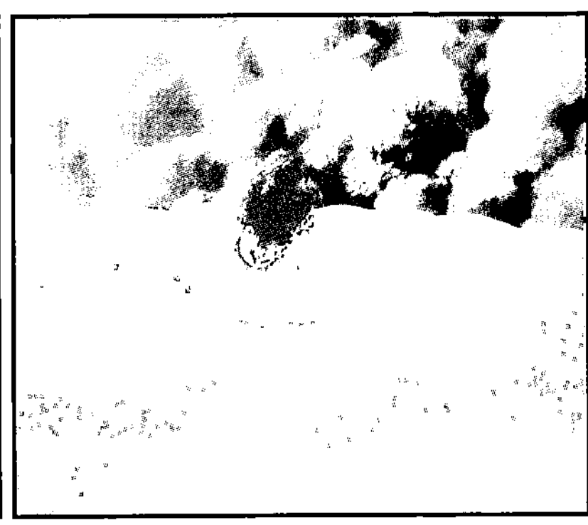

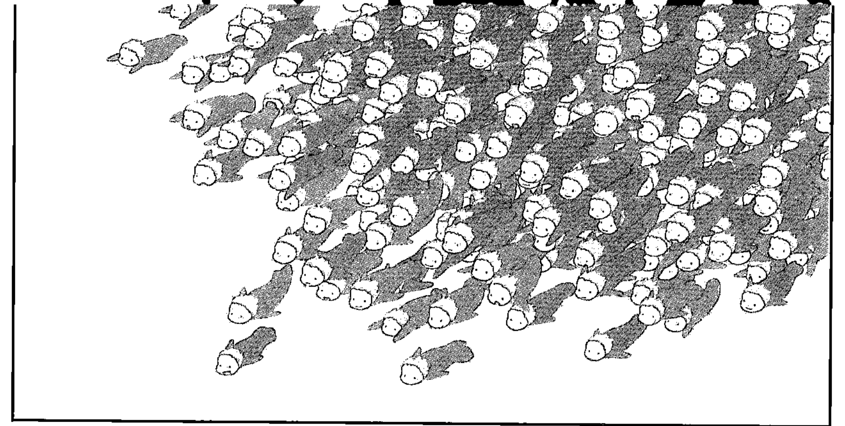

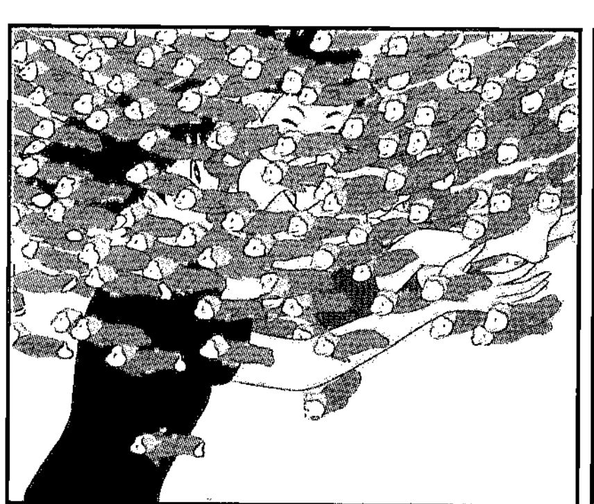

GLP GLP.
(MAMA.)

GLP GLP.
(SOSUKE.)

GLP GLP.
(...?!)

GLP GLP.
(PONYO!)

GLP GLP.
(I'M CONFUSED.)

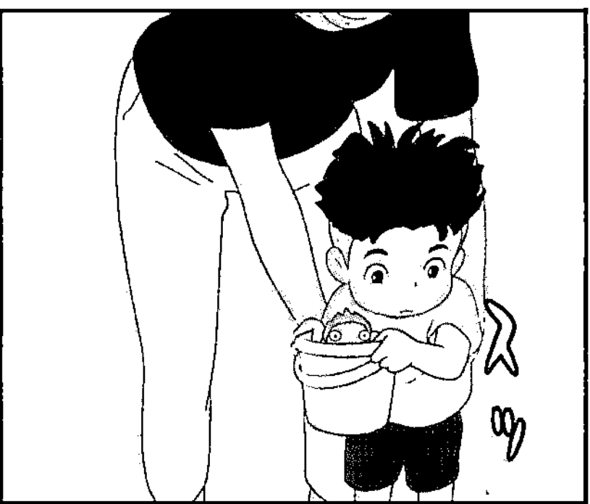

SO THIS IS SOSUKE.

HOW DO YOU DO?

ARE YOU PONYO'S MOTHER?
YES.

YOU BROUGHT MY DAUGHTER SAFELY HERE.
THANK YOU.

SHHHH!

(DO WE KNOW THAT WOMAN ?)

SO-SUKE.
PONYO OPENED A MAGIC WELL BECAUSE SHE WANTS VERY MUCH TO BE HUMAN.

TO BECOME A REAL GIRL...
...SHE NEEDS YOU TO ACCEPT AND LOVE HER AS SHE TRULY IS.

YOU KNOW THAT PONYO WAS A FISH, DON'T YOU?

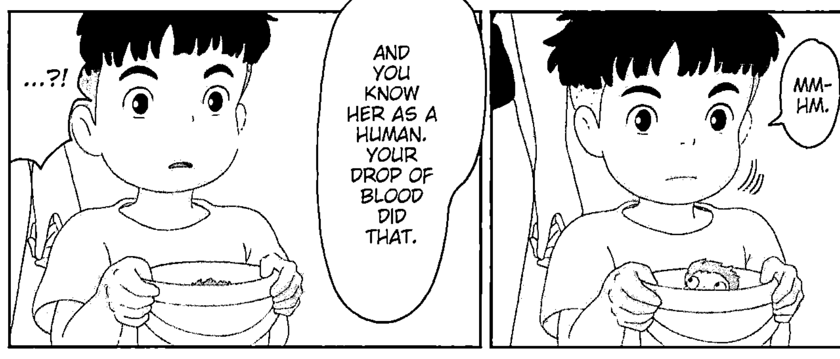
AND YOU KNOW HER AS A HUMAN. YOUR DROP OF BLOOD DID THAT.
...?!
MM-HM.

OH, THAT'S IT?

SO THAT'S HOW SHE CHANGED INTO A HUMAN.

I CUT MY THUMB. THEN PONYO LICKED IT AND MADE IT BETTER.

COULD YOU LOVE HER IF SHE MOVED BETWEEN TWO WORLDS?

MM-HM.
I LOVE ALL THE PONYOS. IT'S A BIG RESPONSIBILITY, BUT...
I LOVE THAT GIRL.

ピョン

クル

スゥ

HA HA HA.

わあっ

PONYO.
COME HERE, PLEASE.

CAN YOU DO THAT?

HM-HM.
コクリ

わあっ

PONYO.
COME HERE, PLEASE.

PONYO.
SOSUKE HAS PROMISED TO ACCEPT YOU AS YOU ARE.

TO BECOME HUMAN, YOU MUST CHOOSE TO ABANDON MAGIC.

CAN YOU DO THAT?

HM-HM.
コクリ

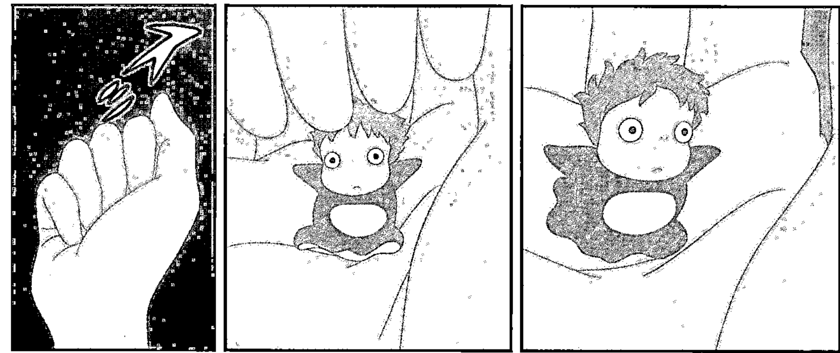

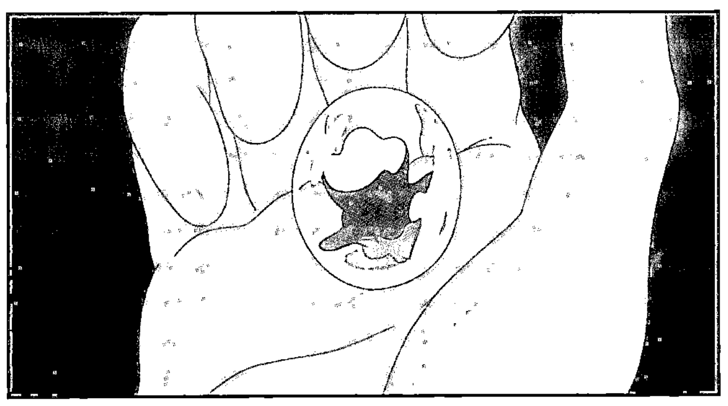

KISS THE BUBBLE, CHILD, WHEN YOU RETURN TO LAND ...

...AND PONYO WILL BECOME A GIRL, GROWING UP JUST LIKE YOU.

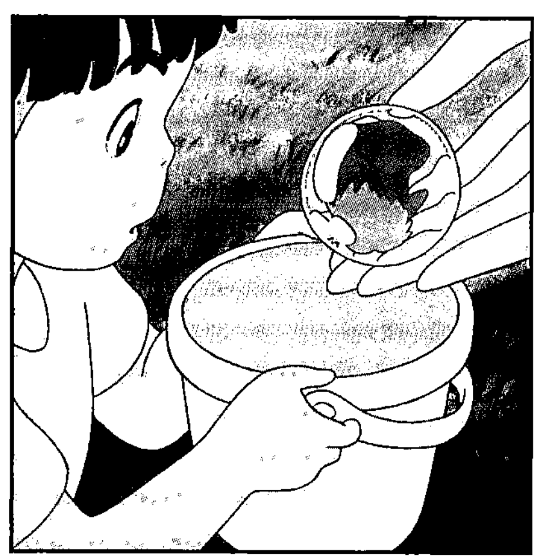

I ACCEPT...
PONYO...

THANK YOU...
PONYO'S MOTHER.

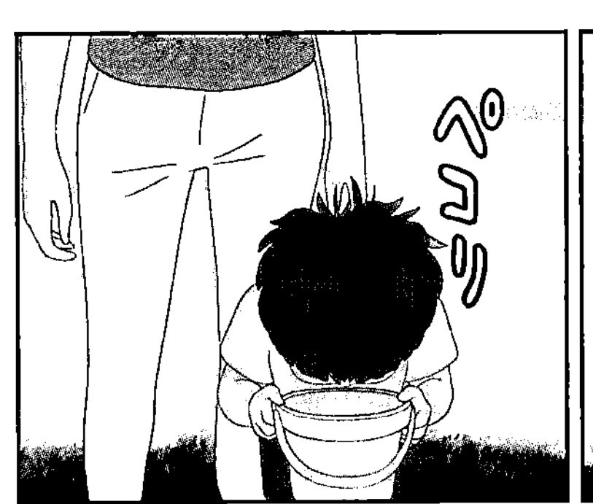
ペコリ

EVERY-ONE!
THE BALANCE OF NATURE IS RESTORED. LIFE BEGINS AGAIN.

わあーっ
HE DID IT!
OF COURSE HE DID!
SO PROUD, SO PROUD.

IT'S SO LOVE-LY.
LISA!
WHAT A RELIEF!

SOSU-KE!

I COULD DIE AND GO TO HEAVEN!
MY GOOD-NESS!

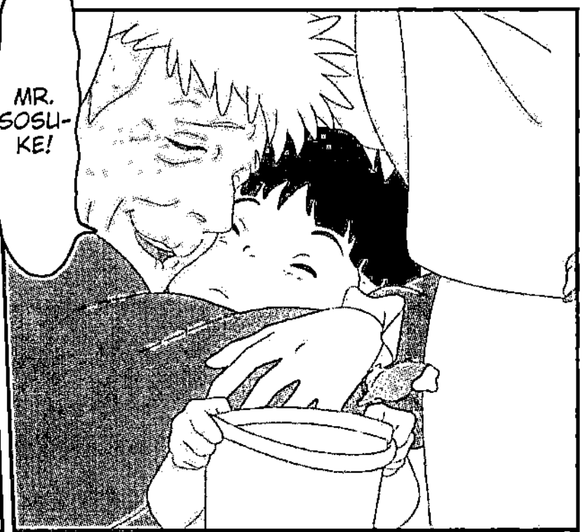
MR. SOSU-KE!

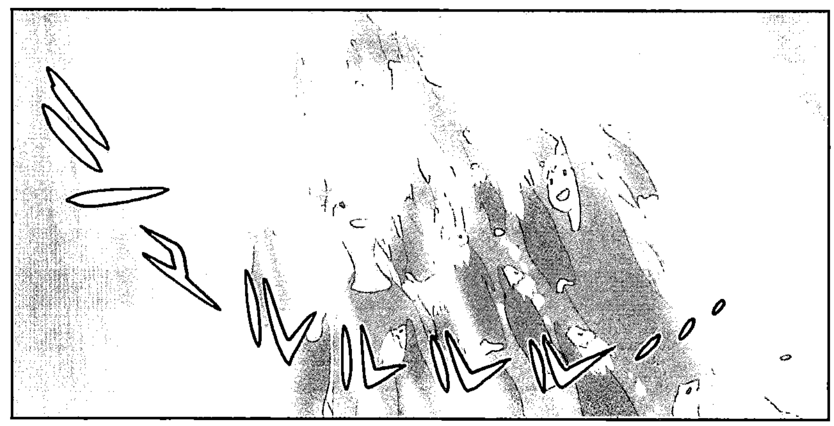

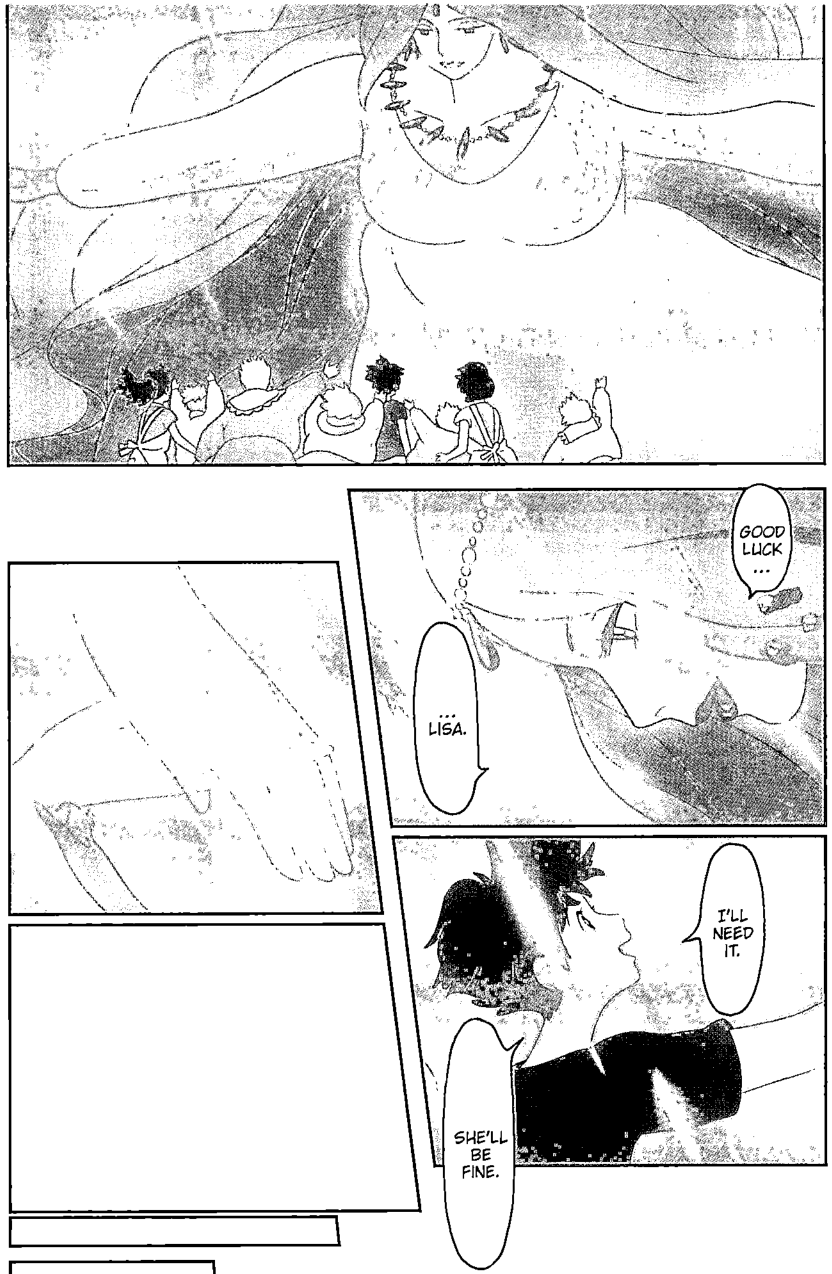
GOOD LUCK ...
... LISA.
I'LL NEED IT.
SHE'LL BE FINE.

THERE YOU ARE!
ARE YOU ALL RIGHT?

WE LIKE TO WALK.
DON'T BOTHER, SHIMA-SAN.

WAIT, I'LL GET THE WHEEL-CHAIRS!

LIFE BEGINS AGAIN.

THIS IS YOURS ...
...I BELIEVE.

OH...
THANK YOU.

REMEMBER ME KINDLY, HMM?
UMMM ...
MAY I?

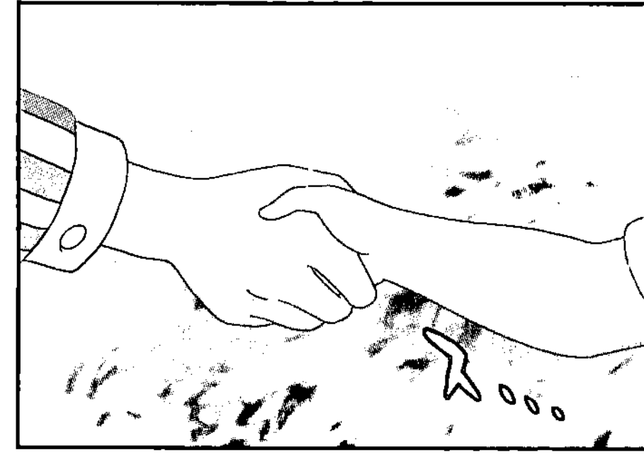

CARE FOR PONYO.

IT'S YOUR DAD!

...!!

プワーー
プワーー

KOICHI!
OVER HERE!
HI!

LISA!
AND SO-SUKE!
AHOY!

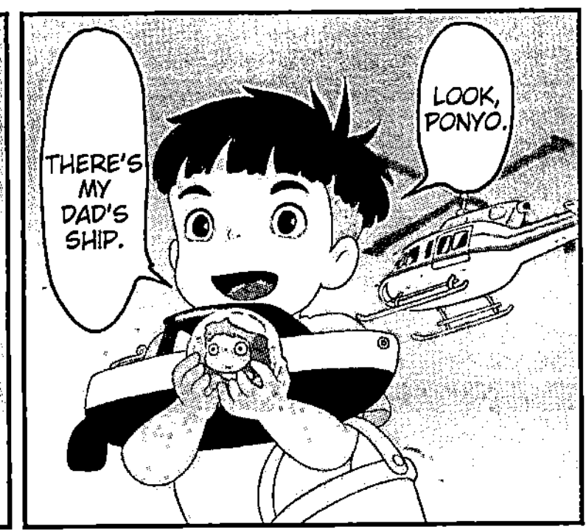
LOOK, PONYO.
THERE'S MY DAD'S SHIP.

HEY!

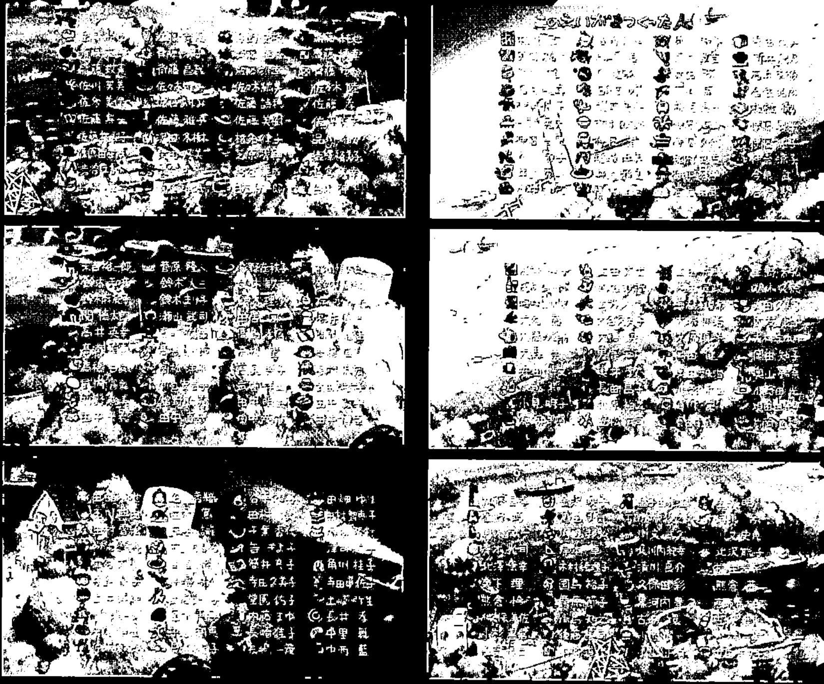

GAKE NO UE NO PONYO

(PONYO ON THE CLIFF OF THE SEA)

When I'm skipping with her, my heart does this dance
Munch n'munch, kiss-hug! Munch n'munch, kiss-hug!
O he's my favorite little boy, rosy-rosy red-red

Ponyo Ponyo Ponyo tiny little fish
She's a little fish from the deep blue sea
Ponyo Ponyo Ponyo she's a little girl
She's a little girl with a round tummy

Sniff-sniff-sniff, this smells so good
I'm so hungry, I'm gonna eat!
Take a look around, very carefully
I'm sure he's there looking too

Ponyo Ponyo Ponyo tiny little fish
She's a little fish from the deep blue sea
Ponyo Ponyo Ponyo she's a little girl
She's a little girl with a round tummy

Pitter-patter, hop-hop and jump
Look, I have legs! I'm gonna run!
Squishy-squeeze, wave them around
Look, I have hands! Let's hold them now!

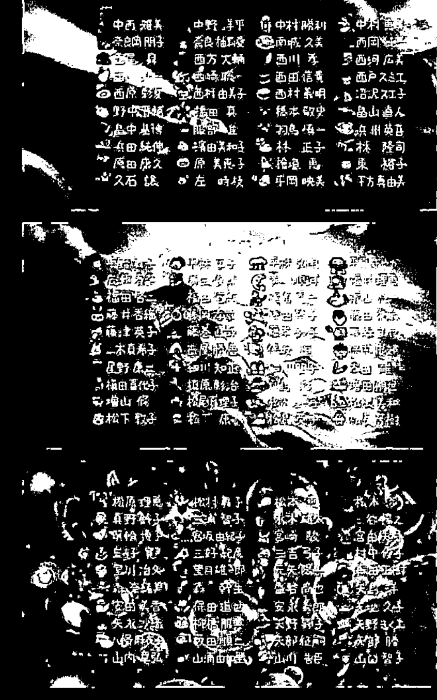

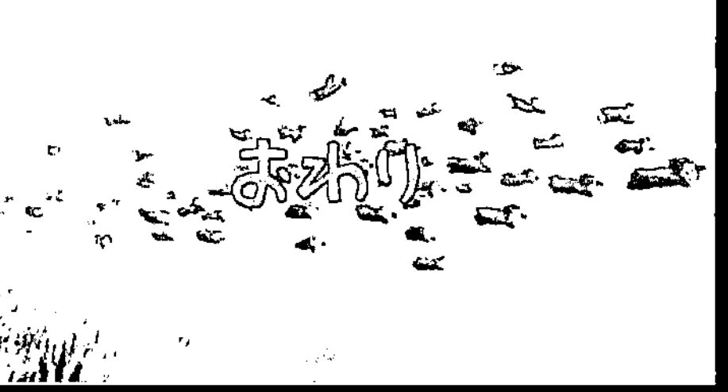

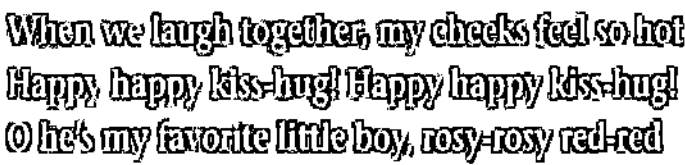

When we laugh together, my cheeks feel so hot
Happy, happy kiss-hug! Happy happy kiss-hug!
O he's my favorite little boy, rosy-rosy red-red

Ponyo Ponyo Ponyo tiny little fish
Came to the house on the cliff by the sea
Ponyo Ponyo Ponyo she's a little girl
She's one happy girl with a round tummy

LYRICS // KATSUYA KONDO
ADDITIONAL LYRICS // HAYAO MIYAZAKI
MUSIC COMPOSITION AND ARRANGEMENT // JOE HISAISHI
PERFORMANCE // FUJIOKA FUJIMAKI & NOZOMI OHASHI
ENGLISH TRANSLATION // RIEKO IZUTSU-VAJIRASARN

Your Guide to *Ponyo* Sound Effects!

To increase your enjoyment of the distinctive Japanese visual style of *Ponyo*, we've included a listing of and guide to the sound effects used in this comic adaptation of the movie. In the comic, these sound effects are written in the Japanese phonetic characters called *katakana*.

In the sound effects glossary for *Ponyo*, sound effects are listed by page and panel number. For example, 4.1 means page 4, panel 1. And if there is more than one sound effect in a panel, the sound effects are listed in order (so, 22.1.1 means page 22, panel 1, first sound effect). Remember that all numbers are given in the original Japanese reading order: right-to-left.

After the page and panel numbers, you'll see the literally translated sound spelled out by the katakana, followed by how this sound effect might have been spelled out, or what it stands for, in English—it is interesting to see the different ways Japanese people describe the sounds of things!

You'll sometimes see a long dash at the end of a sound effects listing. This is just a way of showing that the sound is the kind that lasts for a while; similarly, a hypen and number indicate the panels affected.

Now you are ready to use the *Ponyo* Sound Effects Guide!

5.4 FX: GOCHIN [wham]

6.2 FX: DOTE [thwomp]

7.1 FX: KARARA [roll roll]

12.2 FX: SSU [slp]
12.4 FX: GGU [urr]
12.5 FX: GU GU [grr grr]

13.1-3 FX: AHH [ahh]
13.1.2 FX: BUNYU [blpp]
13.1.3 FX: GI [znn]
13.2.1 FX: BA [boom]
13.2.2 FX: BOOON [womp]
13.3 FX: GOTO [thump]

14.2 FX: NIKAAN [smile]

16.1 FX: GUI [pull]
16.2 FX: DADDA [thmp]
16.3 FX: DA [tmp]

17.1 FX: ZABU ZABU [splish splish]
17.2 FX: BASHAAN [splash]

18.4 FX: HAHAHAHA [ha ha ha]

19.1 FX: SUIII [float]

20.2 FX: SUUU [huppp]
20.3 FX: CHAPU [splsh]

21.2.1 FX: ZABA [plopp]
21.2.2 FX: SUU HAAA SUU HAAA [huff huff huff]
21.3 FX: SUUU [huppp]
21.4 FX: POCHAN [splsh]

22.2 FX: CHAPON [splsh]
22.4 FX: BUUU [fuuuuu]
22.5 FX: BEKON [plupp]

23.1 FX: GOBO [glibb]
23.2 FX: DOBA [blast]
23.3 FX: DOBOBO [boosh boosh]

24.2 FX: CHAPO [splsh]

25.5 FX: DOTA DOTA [thmp thmp]

26.2 FX: GASA [bustle]
26.4 FX: GOSO [shove]

27.2 FX: GGU [grp]
27.3 FX: KIRI [hmph]

28.1 FX: TON [tmp]
28.3 FX: GASA [pick]
28.4 FX: SHUPPA [spark]

29.3 FX: PPA [hpp]
29.6 FX: PPO [glow]

30.3 FX: SSU [push]

31.3 FX: BEKO BEKO BEKO [blpp blpp blpp]
31.4 FX: BEKO BEKO BEKO [blpp blpp blpp]
31.5 FX: BEKO BEKO BEKO [blpp blpp blpp]

32.1 FX: TEKE TEKE TEKE [blip blip blip]
32.2 FX: TEKE TEKE [blip blip]
32.3 FX: TEKE TEKE [blip blip]

33.1 FX: TEKE TEKE TEKE [blip blip blip]
33.2 FX: TEKE TEKE TEKE [blip blip blip]

54.4 FX: TEKE TEKE TEKE [blip blip blip]
54.5 FX: TEKE TEKE [blip blip]

55.3 FX: TEKE TEKE [blip blip]
55.4 FX: TEKE TEKE [blip blip]
55.6.1 FX: HICK HICK [arghh arghh]
55.6.2 FX: UEEEN [waaaaah]

56.1 FX: UEEEN [waaaaah]
56.2 FX: EIYAA EIYAA EIYAA [peer peer peer]
56.3 FX: BIEEE [hyaaaa]
56.5 FX: PA [pop]
56.6 FX: BA [whop]
56.7 FX: BACHA [plish]
56.8 FX: BACHA [plish]
56.9 FX: BACHA [plish]

57.1 FX: TON [thmp]
57.2 FX: TA TA TA [tmp tmp tmp]
57.3.1 FX: DA [whoosh]
57.3.2 FX: UEEEN [whaaa]
57.4 FX: BITA [smack]
57.5.1 FX: GYUUU [squeeze]
57.5.2 FX: GURI GURI [rub rub]

58.1 FX: NIKA [smirk]
58.2 FX: PPA [shpa]
58.3 FX: KYOTON [huh?]
58.4 FX: TA TA TA [tp tp tp]
58.5.1 FX: PYOON [jump]
58.5.2 FX: TA [tmp]

59.1 FX: PASHA PASHA [plish plish]
59.2 FX: PASHA [plish]
59.3 FX: TON [thmp]
59.6 FX: AU AU [aha aha]
59.7 FX: AUU [ghaa]

60.1 FX: TEKE TEKE TEKE [blip blip blip]
60.2 FX: TEKE TEKE TEKE TEKE [blip blip blip blip]

61.4 FX: TEKE TEKE [blip blip]

62.2 FX: SA [hupp]
62.3 FX: TEKE TEKE TEKE [blip blip blip]
62.4 FX: TEKE TEKE TEKE... [blip blip blip...]

64.1.1 FX: KUEEE [kwaaa]
64.1.2 FX: TEKE TEKE TEKE [blip blip blip]

65.1 FX: TEKE TEKE TEKE TEKE TEKE [blip blip blip blip blip]
65.2 FX: TOROON [droop]
65.3 FX: KOKURI [nod]
65.5 FX: GURI GURI [rub rub]

33.4 FX: TEKE TEKE [blip blip]

34.2 FX: TEKE TEKE [blip blip]
34.3 FX: TEKE TEKE TEKE [blip blip blip]
34.4 FX: TEKE TEKE TEKE [blip blip blip]

35.2 FX: TEKE TEKE TEKE [blip blip blip]

39.2 FX: ZAZA [shwa shwa]
39.3 FX: PASHA [splash]
39.4.1 FX: PASHA [splash]
39.4.2 FX: PICHA [splish]

40.4 FX: TEKE TEKE [blip blip]
40.5 FX: TEKE TEKE [blip blip]

41.1.1 FX: TEKE TEKE [blip blip]
41.1.2 FX: GUI [pull]
41.2.1 FX: GUI [pull]
41.2.2 FX: DEKE DEKE [blipp blipp]
41.3 FX: DEKE DEKE [blipp blipp]
41.4 FX: DEKE DEKE DEKE [blipp blipp blipp]
41.5 FX: DEKE DEKE [blipp blipp]
41.5 FX: DEKE DEKE DEKE [blipp blipp blipp]

42.1 FX: SUUU [hppp]
42.2.1 FX: BUUU [fwoooo]
42.2.2 FX: BOWA [woosh]

44.2 FX: FU FU FU [he he he]
44.4 FX: MM [mm hm]

45.2 FX: JIII [stare]

46.5 FX: KOKURI [nod]
46.6 FX: SA [slpp]
46.7 FX: BATA BATA [kick kick]

47.2 FX: SSU [here]

48.4 FX: DOBO DOBO [plopp plopp]
48.5 FX: POTA [drip]

49.4 FX: AU AU [grg grg]

51.3 FX: EII EII EII [paddle paddle paddle]
51.4 FX: EII EII [paddle paddle]

52.1 FX: EIYAA EIYAA [peer peer]

53.5 FX: ZII [zip]

54.1.1 FX: GOSO GOSO [bustle bustle]
54.1.2 FX: EIYAAA [peer]
54.2.1 FX: EIYAA EIYAA [peer peer]
54.2.2 FX: SA [here]

86.2 FX: POTA [drop]
86.3 FX: GOSHI GOSHI [rub rub]
86.4 FX: SSU [slpp]

89.2 FX: HA HA HA [ha ha ha]
89.3 FX: TA TA [tp tp]
89.4.1 FX: TA TA [tp tp]
89.4.2 FX: TA TA [tp tp]

90.1 FX: TA [tmp]
90.4 FX: KYAHAHAHA [ha ha ha ha]

91.3 FX: KYAHAHAHA [ha ha ha ha]
91.4 FX: TA TA TA [tp tp tp]
91.5 FX: DA [tmp]

92.1 FX: DA [tmp]
92.2 FX: TA TA TA [tp tp tp]
92.3 FX: BA [wham]
92.4.1 FX: HA HA HA HA HA HA HA [ha ha ha ha ha]
92.4.2 FX: KYAHAHA [ha ha ha]
92.5.1 FX: KYAAA [ahhh]
92.5.2 FX: HAHAHA [ha ha ha]
92.5.3 FX: AHAHAHA [he he he]

94.1 FX: KYAHAHAHA [ha ha ha]

95.2 FX: SSA [slp]
95.4 FX: SSU [sllpp]
95.5 FX: FUWA [float]

99.2 FX: TA TA [tp tp]

102.5.1 FX: KOTON [blop]
102.5.2 FX: ZURU ZURU [drag drag]

103.3 FX: HENA HENA [wheeee]
103.4.1 FX: KUTA [fwomp]
103.4.2 FX: KOTON [drop]
103.5 FX: SA [haa]

104.1 FX: KUUU [zzzz]
104.3 FX: KUTA [droop]
104.4 FX: KII [glare]
104.5 FX: DA [thmp]

105.1.1 FX: HAA HAA [huff huff]
105.1.2 FX: TA TA TA [tmp tmp tmp]
105.2 FX: HAA HAA [huff huff]
105.2-3 FX: TA TA TA TA TA [tp tp tp tp tp]

106.1 FX: TA TA TA [tp tp tp]
106.2.1 FX: BASHA [splash]
106.2.2 FX: ZABU ZABU [splish splish]

107.1 FX: GOBO GOBO GOBO [blopp blopp blopp]
107.2 FX: KUUU [zzzz]

67.1 FX: SHUN [fwaa]

68.2 FX: SUUU [zzzz]
68.5 FX: FU [haa]

70.1 FX: FURA [fwomp]
70.2.1 FX: POTE [plop]
70.2.2 FX: KUUU [zzzzz]
70.4.1 FX: KUUU [zzzzz]
70.4.2 FX: SUUU [zzzzz]

71.1 FX: CHAPON [splash]
71.3 FX: CHAPU [plosh]
71.5 FX: BASHA BASHA [kick kick]

72.1 FX: BASHA BASHA [kick kick]
72.2 FX: BASHA BASHA [kick kick]
72.3 FX: BASHA BASHA [kick kick]

73.4.1 FX: ZURU [slip]
73.4.2 FX: ZABUNN [splash]
73.5 FX: ZABA [plopp]

75.2-3 FX: PURU PURU [blbb blbb]

76.4.1 FX: ZABU ZABU ZABU [blish blash blash]
76.4.2 FX: HAA HAA [huff huff]

77.1 FX: ZABU [blish]
77.2 FX: HAA HAA [huff huff]
77.3 FX: BASHA BASHA [splash splash]
77.4.1 FX: HAA HAA [huff huff]
77.4.2 FX: BASHA BASHA [splash splash]

78.1 FX: ZURU [drag]
78.2.1 FX: BASHA [splash]
78.2.2 FX: DOTAN [smack]
78.3 FX: DOBON [boom]
78.5.1 FX: KUUU [zzzz]
78.5.2 FX: HAA HAA HAA [huff huff huff]

79.1 FX: SUUU [zzzz]
79.3 FX: GOSHI GOSHI [rub rub]
79.4 FX: FWAAA [yawn]

80.5 FX: HA [hupp]

81.5 FX: TA [tmp]

82.1 FX: TA TA TA [tp tp tp]
82.2 FX: GACHA [chakunk]

83.4 FX: TA TA [tp tp]

85.2 FX: JAAA [pour]
85.4 FX: PETA PETA [plit plat]
85.5 FX: PETA PETA [plit plat]

132.1 FX: HA [hupp]
132.2 FX: SU [slide]

133.2 FX: SU [slp]

138.1 FX: PYON [jump]
138.3 FX: KURU [flip]
138.7 FX: SUUU [bloop]

139.3 FX: WAAA [yay!]

141.2 FX: KOKU [nod]

142.2 FX: KOKURI [nod]
142.5 FX: SU [shwa]

144.1 FX: FUWA [float]

145.3 FX: PEKORI [bow]

146.2 FX: WAAA [yay!]
146.3 FX: TA [tpp]
146.4 FX: TA TA [tp tp]

147.1 FX: BASHI [hug]
147.2.1 FX: BA [hug]
147.2.2 FX: TA TA [tp tp]
147.3.1 FX: GYUUU [squeeze]
147.3.2 FX: HA HA HA [ha ha ha]

148.2 FX: BASHU [waaaa]
148.3 FX: SHURURURURU [twrl twrl twrl twrl]

150.1.1 FX: BA BA BA BA BA [whm whm whm whm whm]
150.1.2 FX: ZA ZA ZA [vmm vmm vmm]
150.2 FX: BA BA BA BA BA [whm whm whm whm whm]

151.4 FX: BA BA BA BA [whm whm whm whm]

152.4 FX: SO [ssu]
152.5 FX: SU [shk]

153.1 FX: BA BA BA [whm whm whm]
153.2 FX: PUWAAA [bwaaaa]
153.4.1 FX: BA BA BA [whm whm whm]
153.4.2 FX: DA [dmp]

154.1.1 FX: PUWAA PUWAA [bwaa bwaa]
154.1.2 FX: TA TA [tp tp]

155.3 FX: PYOON [jump]
155.7 FX: HYUUN [vooom]

156.2 FX: BITAAAN [smack]
156.3 FX: PAAAN [pop]

107.3 FX: YUSA YUSA [shake shake]

110.4 FX: SUUU [shwaaa]

112.2.1 FX: CHAPON [splash]
112.2.2 FX: GGU [grip]

114.2 FX: BBA [wha]

116.1 FX: DA [zoom]
116.2.1 FX: GGU [grip]
116.2.2 FX: CHAPON [splash]
116.3 FX: JI [stare]
116.4 FX: HA [hupp]

117.2 FX: PUUU [spewww]
117.3 FX: BISHAAA [splash]
117.4 FX: BASHA BASHA [plish plish]

118.1.1 FX: HAA HAA [huff huff]
118.1.2 FX: BASHA BASHA [plish plish]
118.2 FX: ZABA [plopp]
118.3.1 FX: HAA HAA [huff huff]
118.3.2 FX: TA TA TA TA [tp tp tp tp]
118.4 FX: CHAPU CHAPU [splish splish]
118.5 FX: TA TA TA [tp tp tp]

119.1 FX: YORO YORO [wobble wobble]
119.2 FX: GAKU GAKU [shake shake]
119.3 FX: ZABU [splosh]
119.4 FX: ZZA [ssa]
119.5 FX: BA [relelase]

120.2 FX: ZA ZA ZA ZA [zoom zoom zoom zoom]
120.3 FX: TA TA TA [tp tp tp]
120.4 FX: TA TA TA [tp tp tp]
120.5 FX: YOTA YOTA [wobble wobble]

121.1 FX: BA [jump]
121.2 FX: FUWA [float]
121.3-4 FX: BASHAA [splash]
121.4 FX: GASHI [grab]

122.1 FX: WAAAA [wooosh]
122.2 FX: POTA [flop]
122.3-4 FX: DOWAAAA [dwooosh]

123.1-2 FX: DOBAAAA [dwoosh]
123.3-4 FX: ZABAAAA [wooosh]

125.5 FX: UMU [hmm]

126.1 FX: SA [slp]
126.2 FX: GU [grr]
126.4 FX: BURU BURUN [blip blip]
126.5 FX: ZAAA [shaaa]

This book should be read in its original Japanese right-to-left format.
Please turn it around to begin!

Volume 4 of 4

Original story and screenplay written and directed by
Hayao Miyazaki

Translated from the original Japanese by Jim Hubbert
English-language screenplay by Melissa Mathison

Film Comic Adaptation/Mai Ihara
Lettering/Rina Mapa
Design/Carolina Ugalde
Editor/Megan Bates
Editorial Director/Masumi Washington

VP, Production/Alvin Lu
VP, Publishing Licensing/Rika Inouye
VP, Sales & Product Marketing/Gonzalo Ferreyra
VP, Creative/Linda Espinosa
Publisher/Hyoe Narita

First published in Japan by Tokuma Shoten Co., Ltd.

Printed in Singapore

Published by
VIZ Media, LLC
295 Bay St.
San Francisco, CA 94133

First printing, September 2009

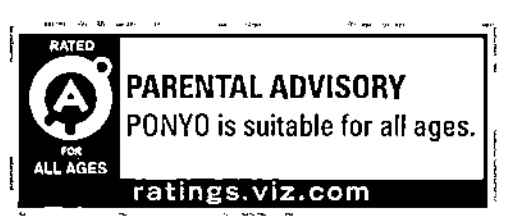